CREATING CUSTOMER LOVE

CREATING CUSTOMER LOVE

Baker College of Clinton Twp Library

Make Your Customers Love You
So Much They'll Never Go Anyplace Else!

DAVE
RATNER

BridgewayBooks

Creating Customer Love: Make Your Customers Love You So Much
They'll Never Go Anyplace Else!
Published by Bridgeway Books
P.O. Box 80107
Austin, Texas 78758

For more information about our books, please write to us, call
512.478.2028, or visit our website at www.bridgewaybooks.net.

LCCN: 2008939304

ISBN-13: 978-1-934454-32-9
ISBN-10: 1-934454-32-X

Front cover design by Bill Eisner

10 9 8 7 6 5 4 3 2 1

I'd like to dedicate this book to my wife Ellen, who patiently and lovingly listens to me fret and complain about the store on a nightly basis, and then shares those tender words: "If you're not going to shut up, could you go sleep in the other room?"

To my three children,
Alison, Andrew, and Douglas

And finally, to the folks who have taught me so much and made my success possible: my employees. You are the ones who are really responsible for my success. I couldn't have done it without you.

Table of Contents

Foreword

Conversations with Dave Ratner are often sprinkled with comments like "I'm such a knucklehead" and "My mistake was—" Such self-analysis comes easily to Dave, who, in over thirty years of retail experience and face-to-face customer contact, has never stopped trying to do things better. Many of the ideas in this book come under the heading of common sense. Others are truly groundbreaking and inspired. Put together, they form a powerful "how-to" for anyone truly interested in improving the customer experience.

If you expand the idea of "customer" to include clients, patients, employees, students, and even friends, Dave's insights apply to *everyone*.

Read this book from cover to cover. Then, read it again. Put some of Dave's ideas to work in your business. You'll enjoy the results!

Michael A. Serafino
March 2, 2008

Acknowledgments

I've been very lucky to have a lot of very smart people in my life, to influence me and guide me, providing inspiration and insight— and, of course, to provide me with not-so-subtle hints, like "When are you gonna write the book already?"

So I'd like to thank BJ Bueno, from Nonbox Consulting, author of *The Power of Cult Branding*; Bill Eisner, of Nonbox Consulting, who reminded me that I've only got thirty years of experience; John Goodman, from Pareto Marketing for his support and encouragement; Mike Goldsmith, a fellow pet store owner; Rick Segel, one of the best retail speakers I've ever heard; Michael Serafino, who was so eager to see this book he even wrote prospective chapter titles for me; Cindy Potts, for ensuring the book arrived before my great-grandchildren did; and Mort Brown, co-author of *So You Want to Own Your Own Store*, for all his encouragement.

A special thank you goes out to A. O. White, my first employer, and the man who taught me how I wanted to run my own business. Everything I learned, I learned from him. He taught me the value of treating the customer better than they'd be treated anywhere else.

Introduction:

Welcome to Dave's!

We'll start right off with who this book is not for:

This book is not going to help you if you're Wal-Mart. This book is for the small business owner—and let's face it, unless you're Wal-Mart or the federal government, you're running a small business.

That's all right. The chances are you're not Wal-Mart, and I'm pretty sure you're not the federal government. Chances are you're just like me: a guy who either owns a store or two, is a salesperson, or runs a business. You have a passion for your customers and the need to compete in an environment where it seems like the big guy always wins, no matter what.

Why are the big guys winning? Sometimes it's just a matter of scale; when you've got a gazillion-dollar purchasing budget and enough clout to sway the product designs of major manufacturers, you get a competitive edge. Larger retailers can advertise more, pay more for the best locations, and more often than not, undercut prices to a degree that no independent retailer can match.

That's the bad news—but there's good news, too! So we'll never beat the big guys on price. That's okay. We've got our own advantages. Because we're small, independent retailers, we're flexible and able to respond quickly and effectively to every changing customer demand. We can offer a level of personal service the big guys can only dream about.

In short, we can make our customers love us.

That's really great news, because I believe, just like all the great philosophers and musicians (not necessarily in that order) that love conquers all. If we have customers who love us, love us so much that they'd never dream of going anywhere else, then we'll be able to compete with the mega retailers—compete and win!

There are a lot of folks like us. That gives me a lot of hope, because I'm passionate about independent business. I love it when the little guy beats the snot out of the big guy, and I'm guessing you do, too.

It can be done. I know it can be done (and this is going to sound obnoxious, but we might as well get it out of the way right now that sometimes I'm a little obnoxious) because I've been doing it for over thirty years. Dave's Soda and Pet City is only four stores, yet we hold our own against the PETCOs, the warehouse superstores, Internet sites, and more.

We do it, and you can do it, too. Everything you're going to find in this book is real-life experience, tested on the front lines, and put to the test day in and day out, for years. If it's in this book, it works.

A lot of this stuff is common sense. Entrepreneurs generally have a great deal of common sense. They understand what works and what doesn't. At the end of the day, we know our success is providing what our customers want. The trick is discovering what they want and delivering it in such a way that they don't want to get it anywhere else. Our customers have to love us. That's how we beat Wal-Mart. That's how the little guy carries the day. It's the power of love.

I go on the road a lot, and speak to independent business owners. While you're reading this book, I want you to view it like a speech. In here, you'll find those nuggets of wisdom that will totally transform your business. At the end of each chapter, you'll find Dave's Dozen, which encapsulates what was covered in that section. It's a great place to pick one or two things you want to start trying immediately. Life will get better, your business will grow, and you'll be a happy camper. I guarantee it. If not, you'll get your money back.

Who is this Dave guy anyway?

If I have to say I'm anything, and I do, or this would be a really short introduction, I'd have to say I've always been a funny guy, and I've always been an entrepreneur. Of course, my technique wasn't always as refined as it is now. No one starts out knowing everything, after all, and I did a lot of learning on the go. My business education started early.

Growing up, all the kids in my neighborhood had to go to catechism, Hebrew school, or some other form of after-school torture. I had to go to Hebrew school. Every day, they'd have a snack for the kids: chocolate milk and cookies. No problem, right?

Then they stopped serving chocolate milk. It was just regular milk and cookies from then on. So I did what any sensible entrepreneur would do: I went and bought a container of Nestlé's Quik and sold scoops of the magic chocolate powder for twenty-five cents each.

That didn't go over quite as well as I had planned.

Still, that background of humor and entrepreneurship has stood by me. I've been able to do some amazing things. In 1975, I rented a three-bay gas station and started selling all different kinds of soda out of there. It was a great little business.

A few years later, I bought a dog. You've got to feed a dog, so I went to the grocery store. That's where I had an epiphany: I was standing there, looking down the aisles, and said "Holy Smokes! There's more pet food in here than there is soda!" Everybody drinks soda. Everyone has a pet. Dave's Soda and Pet City was born.

It's been a fabulous journey. The pet side of the business grew and grew from there, until now soda makes up only 4 percent of the business we do. We're known as a "giant-killer"—an independent retailer who can stand up to the chains and win!

I sit on the board of the Retail Advertising and Marketing Association, right next to the CMOs and VPs from Kohls, Target, and PetSmart (believe me, *that* gets interesting). It's all these big guys and me. I got to testify in front of the Senate Finance Committee about the state of independent retailing, and you'd better believe that was a trip. Yours truly has been featured in the *Wall Street Journal*, the *New York Times*, and by the Associated Press. We've shown up on the *NBC National News* twice! But perhaps the honor I'm most proud of is that my mini-chain of stores, Dave's Soda and Pet City, is the habitual winner of the "Best Of" designation, voted on by area residents and featured in *The Valley Advocate*, our alternative community newspaper.

How do we do it?

Nothing we do is rocket science. It's all duplicable: you can do the same exact things in your business, if you really want to do them. You need a good crew, and the ability to commit yourself to great customer service, but it can be done.

There are a lot of things you need to have if you want to run a successful business. You need a great location, convenient and easily accessible. You need the right services or merchandise and a knowledgeable staff that's friendly, easy to work with, and great at selling your stuff. You also need the ability to identify what the public wants and present it to them in an enticing fashion.

You can have all of these things and still have a failing business if you're missing one essential element: loyal customers. Customer loyalty is the make-or-break component in your success. Every retailer wants to hear that the customer comes back because you're "their" store. Every accountant wants to be their client's "people." Every business needs a clientele that identifies with and values it.

So how do you get customer loyalty? How do you, in short, make your customers love you so much that they feel too guilty to go anyplace else?

Customers are funny. They'd like to be loyal, they really would. But there are so many reasons for them to stray—to other retailers, to online vendors, to other service professionals, you name it. Customers are only loyal to you as long as certain, specific things happen. From the minute customers first encounter your business, whether that's in person, online, or through advertising and word of mouth, you've got a limited number of opportunities to build and reinforce your relationship with them. Understanding what these opportunities are and making the most of them builds that loyalty.

There are no guarantees. That's not news to you as a business owner. You know you can do everything right, and the competitor who does everything wrong will still get the sale because their location is near your customer's workplace and yours is not. People's lives are changing, and whoever has the most convenient business usually wins. That being said, there are real, concrete things you can do to make yourself not only the most convenient business, but the most beloved, loyalty-inspiring business.

How to use this book

Creating Customer Love contains everything you need to know to start creating customer love in your stores. Bear in mind that each store is different and every retailer will have his or her own approach. What you're holding in your hands is a starting point, a guide you can use to begin to create a unique customer experience in your stores. Adapt and refine what you find here until it works perfectly for you!

The book is divided into three parts. In part 1, I'll talk about customer service and the role it has in creating customer love. This section will cover everything from creating a store promise and delivering on it, to cultivating a customer-first attitude and implementing damage control policies. In part 2, I'll cover your crew: the employees who make your store great. I'll discuss everything from who to hire to how to involve employees so that they're invested in your company. I'll also explain what to do when you have to let someone go. In part 3, I'll talk about how to make your store a great place to be, from the layout to the day-to-day operations. This section includes information on advertising, sales, and returns.

At the end of each section, you'll find Dave's Dozen, a short checklist of points you can start using immediately to make your store better. (Sharp-eyed readers might notice that each Dave's Dozen contains thirteen items—an example of always delivering more than you promise!)

Part One:

Unless You're The Cheapest Place on the Planet, You Need to Offer a Great Shopping Experience

The retailer who lives by price dies by price! That's pretty well-established. If you doubt me, take a look at any of the hundreds of defunct stores that tried to compete head to head with mega retailers and kept cutting their prices. They cut their prices so much, they went out of business.

To succeed as a retailer in this competitive world, we've got to change the game. We can't wage price wars and win. Instead, we've got to focus on the shopping experience. The time our customers spend with us has to fulfill their expectations for a great time. That's how we create customer love.

Chapter 1:

Understanding
the Customer Experience

Customer service is not the toothless greeter at Wal-Mart. Customer service is not big signs that say "We care about customer service!" Customer service isn't any of the millions of gimmicks and trappings business owners try to hang on the concept.

Customer service is one simple thing: the customer experience. Everything the customer experiences while visiting your business makes up that experience:

> Did they find you easily?
> Could they park without difficulty?
> Can clients reach you easily—one phone call to get a real person?
> Is it easy to walk into the business, or do they have to turn sideways to make their way through outdoor displays positioned too close to the entryway?
> Are they greeted by your happy, upbeat, friendly employees or a bunch of teenagers who'd obviously rather be anywhere else right now?
> Does the merchandise appeal to them?
> Do you have the merchandise the customer expects to find in stock?
> Do you offer a wide variety of merchandise?
> Is there always something new to look at, or is it the same-old, same-old?
> Can they find what they came for easily?
> Are prices in keeping with what the customer expected to pay?

> ➤ If they need help making choices, is someone there to explain the difference between items?
> ➤ Are the checkout lines short?
> ➤ Does the cashier smile, engage with them, and ring up the order quickly?
> ➤ Does someone offer to carry the order to the car?
> ➤ What happens if they need to return the merchandise?

These are just a few questions you must ask yourself. There are more—some minor, some major, but all important to the customer asking them. If the customer likes the answers you provide to the questions—if they enjoy their experience—chances are they'll be back. Drop the ball here, though, and you're done.

Sometimes the smallest things have the largest impact. It's kind of hard to swallow, for a lot of business owners, but it's true: those "little" things that you might not pay much attention to can have a tremendous impact on your customer's decision to return.

For example, let's say you're running a sale on one of your most popular items. You advertise well and draw in a lot of traffic. Your customer comes to the store, finds an attractively signed and merchandised display of the item, at a great price, and snatches it up. Then she gets up to the checkout line where practically everyone in the world is also waiting to be checked out by a gum-snapping teenager who's too busy talking with a cute stock boy to ring up purchases in anything close to a timely fashion.

So what does your customer do? She looks at the long line. She looks at the item in her hand. She looks at her watch. She does some mental calculations, and she decides that the savings on the item she'd get buying it now isn't worth the time and aggravation of waiting in line. She puts the item down and walks out of your store.

That's a lost sale. That's bad enough. It gets even worse (or better, if you want to look at it from your competition's point of view). The next time you run a sales event, this customer might look over the flyer and remember her experience. She's not going to come back, because she didn't have a good experience. Worse, she'll tell her friends and co-workers about the long lines and horrible cashier, and some of them will listen to her and also avoid your store. One negative customer experience has turned this customer off of your business.

If, on the other hand, the experience your customer has matches what your customer expects, you'll be in pretty good shape. This is sort of the "baseline level" of customer service: you promise a certain type of experience, and you deliver a certain type of experience. Taking it to the next level requires not only meeting your customer's expectations of their experience but surpassing them. Focusing on what your customer experiences and doing what you can to make it a positive interaction throughout is the foundation of excellent customer service.

The five dimensions of the customer experience

The customer experience really takes in every dimension of your business. Ideally, everything about your company should make the customer feel good about being there. We're multi-dimensional beings, and we engage with the world on a number of levels. Yet too many business owners totally forget this; they focus on what looks good but drop the ball in other areas.

Let's look at the retail world for a minute here. There's been a tremendous amount of research done in this area, and it's too good to ignore. Bear in mind, though, that the lessons here translate into almost every other type of business. These principles hold true whether you're running a bowling alley or a financial services firm.

Some of this is going to sound like really simplistic, absolute no-brainer stuff, but that retailing research tells us these are some of the primary reasons customers choose not to return to stores. Each reason is tied with a specific sense; if you're going to provide a great customer experience, you've got to make sure that your business caters to the customer on all of these levels:

Sight

A store should look clean, well-lit, and inviting. An organized and convenient layout can do more to drive business than anything else. Color choice and graphic design should appeal to your customer base and accurately reflect your brand.

Sound

Background music should match the tastes of your target audience. If you're a teen apparel store, you need the current popular music; however, that might be totally out of place if you're a bookstore, a jeweler, or an office supply warehouse.

Noisy operations—such as key cutting, pet grooming, and children's craft areas—should be contained in relatively soundproof settings to minimize their impact on other customers.

If you do a lot of business over the phone, you want to make sure the people answering the phone have pleasant, bubbly voices.

Smell

Scents, smells, and odors can have a tremendous impact on your business. Trust me, I run a chain of pet stores. If you think I don't worry about how my stores smell, you've got another thing coming. Bad smells can ruin your store faster than anything else.

Sometimes it's the merchandise you have to worry about. If you've got live creatures as merchandise, you've got an obvious source of—shall we say scents?—to be concerned about. Even pleasant-smelling merchandise, such as candles, body washes, and similar items, can give off an overwhelming wall of scent, to the point where they can turn customers off. If you specialize in this type of product, you're going to want to make sure you have adequate ventilation so your customers can breathe easy.

Every now and then, you're going to have a crew member who's the problem. Some douse themselves with way too much perfume, while others seem to have missed the concept of soap along the way. Take them aside, have a private word, and if they don't get it, and quick, let them go.

Taste

Taste is completely unimportant in some businesses and absolutely crucial in others. If you put out free samples of food and beverages, make sure they're fresh and taste good! This could be something as minor as the little dish of mints you have on the service desk: every now and then someone should taste those and make sure they're not nasty. Not sure of your own tastes? Give one to a kid. Kids will let you know what they think in no uncertain terms.

Touch

One of the few advantages that brick-and-mortar businesses have over online vendors is the fact that customers can come in and actually touch the merchandise. This is actually a huge deal; if you're buying a suit, you want to feel the fabric it's made of—feel the weight and assess the quality. The same thing holds true for dozens and dozens of other categories; yet too often retailers make it difficult for customers to actually touch the merchandise. You're a store, not a museum. Make it possible for your customers to feel what they're considering purchasing. This will obviously require some security precautions in some cases, but the expense will be offset by the advantage you gain catering to this aspect of the customer experience.

Stretching a bit, touch can also encompass feel, and that relates to the interior temperature in your stores. You don't want it to be too hot or too cold. Customers aren't going to stay if they're not comfortable!

The customer experience must match the expectation

I want you to stop for a moment and think back to the last time you went to Costco, Sam's Club, BJ's, or another warehouse superstore. Were you greeted at the door by a finely dressed greeter, wearing a tux and a red carnation? Did someone escort you through all the aisles, pointing out finely merchandised products, carefully arranged into artistic masterpieces? Were you treated as the most important person in the world? Was the entire experience an aesthetic delight?

Of course not! This is Costco. Merchandise towers to the ceilings, and you've got a huge cart to wheel through the aisles on your own as you seek out fifty-gallon jugs of ketchup. There's a minimum of froufrou; little attention is paid to window dressing or merchandising—they cut the wrap off the pallets, and that's about it.

Do you mind that? No, you don't, and there's a reason why. The experience you had at Costco matched your expectation of the experience. Costco delivered exactly what they promised: quality merchandise, at reasonable prices, in a bright, pleasant setting. They never promised to wait on you hand and foot, and you don't expect that from Costco. The fact that there's often a friendly, helpful salesperson around to help you if you need it is pure bonus: it makes the Costco experience better, but it's not an essential element of Costco.

On the other hand, if you go for a custom-made tailored suit, you come to that transaction with certain expectations. You expect to get a great deal of attention. Someone's going to measure you, discuss clothing options with you, and help you slide your arms into the suit jacket—even though you're more than capable of putting on a suit jacket, and may, in fact, have done so on a daily basis for years.

The same scenario holds true for women when they buy couture or high-end clothing. If you ever want to see the ultimate in full-service retail, watch a woman shopping for her wedding dress. There are boutiques that will have sales associates hold the mirror up for you so you can view the back of the neckline without having to move more than your eyes. Over the top? Perhaps. Necessary? I'd say absolutely—because that's the expectation the customer has for that type of purchase, from that type of retailer.

You can't swap them out. The full service boutique experience doesn't translate well to the Costco scenario. That's okay. Neither way of doing business is better or worse than the other. Each has its place, as long as it matches the customer's expectations. There is a place in this world for McDonald's. There is also a place in this world for the fancy gourmet restaurant. The trick is knowing which one you are and making sure you clearly communicate that to the customer.

If there's a disconnect between the customer's expectations and the customer's experience, you're going to have problems. Your primary role as a business owner is to ensure that the customer experience and the customer expectations match.

That being said, it's important to remember that you can always surpass customer expectations. The friendly salespeople at Costco are one example. The bridal boutique that offers dress preservation after the big day is another. Always keep your eyes open for those opportunities to do a better job. Just never forget that you have to make sure you're meeting expectations before you worry about surpassing them!

The nuts and bolts of the customer experience

Now, if you're anything like me, you might be asking, "How does all this stuff about experience and expectation translate into my store?" There are real, tangible, nuts and bolts types of things we can start doing immediately to improve the experience our customers have while they're shopping with us.

There has been tons and tons of research on this, about a gazillion and two special reports and books and articles. You could sit down and start reading all this stuff, but on the off chance you've got a store to run in the meantime, let's touch on the high points.

Obviously, we want to concentrate on the most important topics first. Here are some of the critical things customers look at when they walk into your store:

> Cleanliness
> Paint and wall finishes
> Fixtures, shelving, and lights
> Amount of clutter

Let me bring you into my store for a minute. We sell pets, so our customers expect that we have healthy animals. That brings its own special set of expectations: spotless cages, humane treatment of the animals, and a knowledgeable staff that cares about animals. No one ever tells us they expect this of us—they just do. It's a given that we have to provide these things. Other expectations that are never articulated yet are critically important include the following:

> well-lit store and parking area
> merchandise signed with descriptions and prices
> name tags on every employee
> clean, attractive bathrooms, especially if you cater to children or women
> clean, attractive changing rooms

Local businesses and customer service

There's good news and bad news when it comes to being a local business and customer service. The good news is this: all things being equal, people like to do business with the local guy. It makes them feel good. They like to keep their money in their hometown, rather than send it off to corporate headquarters halfway across the country.

That's the good news: being local gives customers a reason to buy from you. The bad news is that customers expect more from the local guy. If you're a local retailer, you need to provide better service, better merchandise, better product knowledge, and flat out better treatment than your larger competitors. If you're a service provider, you not only have to be as competent and attractively priced as online or national vendors, but you have to know your clientele better than they know themselves.

Is that fair? Absolutely not. Too bad. That's how it is. If you're going to benefit by being a local company, you're also going to pay for it, to some extent. You've got to outperform your larger competitors. You need to give better customer service. You have to have better merchandise, and know more about it. You need to treat your local customers better than the large chains ever dream of doing.

It can be done. Chains know the value of superior customer service, but 99.9 percent of them don't have the budgets to do it. The very way large retailers are structured prevents them from doing the things we, as smaller, independent, local retailers can do. Can you imagine the headaches Wal-Mart would have if they required their employees to carry each and every purchase to the parking lot for their customers? It would be a logistical nightmare. But we can, and our customers love it.

Without knowing what specific business you're in, it's hard for me to tell you what actions constitute great customer service for you. It might be the laundromat sewing the button that falls off of the shirt, or the apparel store calling all their customers when the new spring line arrives. It could be the follow up phone call to make sure a customer's new stereo is working perfectly. It could be the accountant who e-mails clients with updates about the new tax legislation and what it means to them. The actions follow from the attitude that making the customer's experience wonderful is the most important thing. Ask yourself what you can do to make the customer thrilled about doing business with you. The answers to those questions constitute great customer service.

We can be the beacon: that shining light on the hill that sets the standard. We can be the example. We can be the companies that other organizations measure themselves against. We can win the day—if we provide excellent customer service.

Dave's Dozen

1. Customer service is the customer experience; the better the experience, the better the customer perceives the service to be.
2. The customer experience includes everything about your store, your merchandise, and your crew.
3. The experience has to meet the expectation.
4. Your customer experience is your brand. Period.
5. Customers want things to be easy. Is it easy to shop in your store?
6. Be willing to look at every aspect of your store to see how you can make it better.
7. There are five dimensions to the customer experience, and every one of them is important.
8. Customers have long memories; screw up once, and you'll never see them again.
9. Being a local retailer is a blessing and a curse; customers prefer to do business with local companies, but they expect more of them.
10. Customer service is one way the small, independent retailer can position themselves against the chain stores and succeed.
11. Every independent business has unique opportunities to compete with larger competitors: consider what *you* can do that, for reasons of sheer volume, *they* cannot.
12. Don't be afraid to be who you are; there's room in this world for the fast food joint and the fine dining restaurant.
13. We can set the standard when it comes to customer service.

Chapter 2:

Knowing Exactly
Who Your Customers Are

Use your customer knowledge to create a great business

If you want to have a great business, you need to know and understand your customers. One of the best examples I've ever seen of this concept in action is a store called Kiddlywinks, a high-end toy store owned by my friend Joy Leavitt.

Joy has two stores, and it's clear she put a lot of thought into designing the stores to give her target customers a wonderful experience. It starts outside in the parking area: certain spots are reserved for customers with little kids. The staff at Kiddlywinks are young people who obviously enjoy being around children. Everything in the store is set up to be kid-friendly: shelves are lower, the merchandise can be touched, and everything is safer than safe.

The store doesn't try to be all things to all people. It's targeted at a niche audience: parents who want high-end educational toys for their kids. You're not going to find violent video games or discount crayons here: neither would appeal to Joy's market, and she doesn't bother with anything that doesn't. Kiddlywinks does a fabulous amount of business, because Joy obviously understands her customers and goes out of her way to provide the experience they're looking for. That's something we can all do. Small touches can make a big difference.

Barnes & Noble and Borders do a fantastic job with this, as well. Having couches in the store—not to mention a café—is just brilliant. It invites customers to stay and linger, browsing through the books and other merchandise. If you want to listen to a CD before you buy it, they have the technology in place to allow you to listen to sample tracks for every single CD in the store! They went out of their way to make life easy for the customer, by pondering what would make their target audience happy.

I could go on and on with this topic, detailing the innovative ways retailers use their understanding of their customer to create a great experience. Dick's Sporting Goods, a national chain retailer, offers indoor skating rinks in some of their locations for customers to try out skates. Countless music stores let the customers try out the instruments and invite musicians to drop in for impromptu performances and jam sessions. These techniques allow you to connect with a customer on an emotional level. If your kid had a great time skating around Dick's indoor rink, you're going to want to go back to that store again to have more fun. If you were at the music store when a favorite band came in to play, you'll drop back in again in hopes of another performance. It's one more attraction to bring your customer back.

Knowing your customers

You have to really know who your customers are. Understanding who your customers are on a basic, grassroots level will help your marketing. You'll be able to reach out to your customers—and people like your customers—in a very effective way, saving you time and money. Customers who are baby boomers, for example, are very, very different than customers who are twentysomethings. You have to know who's coming to you, and, more importantly, what type of people they are.

In our stores, we've figured out that we've lost the Wal-Mart shopper. We're never going to appeal to the customer who wants the lowest-priced item, all the time. There's no sense chasing that customer, because a) we're never going to get him and b) we'll go broke trying. Instead, we looked closely at the customers who stayed with us, even after the Wal-Marts and Pet Food Warehouses and other superstores set up shop. We discovered that our customers want the good quality products, but they also enjoy getting a really good deal.

That leads me to another important point: never make assumptions about your customers, based on their social status or income levels. One of the most fascinating things I've ever done, and one that's given me real insight into who my customers are and what's important to them, is to go to online demographic websites. These websites track just about everything about the public, from family size to buying habits. The amount you can learn will blow your mind.

At the web site for the US Department of Labor (www.bls.gov/bls/demographic.htm), you can search for demographic data by region, state, and in some cases, neighborhoods. It's a free site and a great place to get started.

On the website for NPD (www.npd.com), perhaps the premier consumer data-tracking research firm in the world, you can check out services aimed specifically at retailers, broken down by category. You pay for the information, but it's well worth it in many cases.

Anyway, back to the point: One thing that really, really surprised me when I first went into business was that the more financially well-off my customers were, the more they enjoyed finding a great deal. These are also the customers who are most likely to use coupons. Want to test this theory? Go to any Costco and look around the parking lot. What type of cars do you see? A lot of BMW's and Volvos, that's what. These are not inexpensive cars. They're driven by people who, by and large, make a great deal of money. And where are these people? They're in Costco, pricing out the Frosted Flakes!

We have four stores. Each one of these stores is in a different income bracket. Consistently, the highest rates of coupon redemption come from the store frequented by those customers who have the highest income levels. Similarly, customers who are well-off are also the most rabidly zealous members of frequent buyer programs, loyalty clubs, and other rewards programs. If you have a program in which you can collect points in order to get something for free, or a buy twelve, get the thirteenth free, you'll discover that most of your club members are those individuals who are the wealthiest.

There's no upper cut-off limit for this phenomenon, either. Neiman Marcus has one of the most sought after points programs in the world. You've got to spend about a zillion dollars in their jewelry department to earn your reward, but when they let people know that all purchases made on a given day will earn triple points, the cash registers start ringing. The biggest fans of low-fee, discount brokerages are the investors with the largest portfolios, far more often than you might expect.

This just goes to show the difference between really knowing your customer and assuming you know your customer.

Identifying your best customers

One of the most important elements of knowing your customers is knowing which customers are the most loyal. Later on, I'll be talking about treating your best customers better, but first you've got to figure out who your best customers are. Most retailers, especially those who have a single store, could probably name two or three of their best customers off the top of their heads, but you need to know more than that. To be effective, you need quantifiable, qualitative data.

Most Point of Sale cash register systems (I'm going to call them POS systems throughout the book) can help you capture and track customer data. If your system isn't currently doing this, chances are there are modules you can purchase that will do this. Check with your vendor about this capability. More than one retailer has discovered, much to their chagrin, that their current POS system was more than adequate to the task; they simply needed to learn how to use the appropriate functions!

If you don't have a POS system, you still need to capture customer data. This will be a little harder, and you'll have to exert a little extra effort, but you still have to do it. Capturing customer data without a POS system can be done by offering some sort of incentive in exchange for the information. Typical incentives include the following:

> contest or drawing for a prize
> a newsletter, with coupons
> loyalty, frequent buyer, or preferred customer card

If you're collecting data manually, you'll want to begin with the most essential information: contact information and identifying data. What type of customers are they? You'll have all this information written down in notebooks, and small slips of paper, and whatnot where, by and large, it's completely useless to you. Call up the local community college and see if you can find a student who will, for a few bucks, come over and set it all up in spreadsheets for you. You need to be able to work with the information for it to have any value. (If you're wondering why I recommend a college student for this task, it's because it's what I would do if I were in that situation. I'm in the breakdown lane on the information superhighway, and if you're in the same spot I'm in, it's well worth it to hire someone to do this for you rather than attempt to do it all yourself!)

Collecting all of this data manually is a lot of work, so I'd strongly urge you to invest in a POS system that tracks this information for you. It's an investment that will pay for itself ten times over.

Get out of the office

Database management can help you discover the nuts and bolts stuff about your customers, but you've also got to get out there and talk with your customers. Don't hide out in the office, cowering behind the computer screen. You'll never get a feel for who's doing business with you and what they value unless you get to know your customers.

Make a point of getting on the floor and talking with the customer. That's one of the prime advantages of being an independent business owner. We get to do that! Do you think the head of Sears is, right now, while you're reading this, on the floor talking to a customer about the relative merits of given chop saws? Of course he's not. Chances are he's in a meeting.

When you're on the floor, you can ask your customers what you can do better. I do this all the time. What do my competitors do better than I do? What merchandise do they carry that I don't? What service do they provide that we don't? Act on what your customers tell you. If I hear that my customers are going to PETCO to buy Sparky's Pet Treats, I'm going to start carrying Sparky's Pet Treats. They're going to buy the product, so I'd much rather they bought it from me.

Spending time with your customer also gives you a sense of who they really are. We sometimes have idealized visions of who our customers are: there's nothing like actually talking with our customers to shatter those myths and put us squarely in the real world. That's good, because we have to make real-world decisions with real-world money.

I've actually just come back from a seminar that gave me a great question to ask my customers: Would you recommend my business to your friends? Why or why not?

You have to fix the why nots; listen to what your customers tell you. This will pay for the book, ten times over: you can't find more targeted, relevant market research than that which comes directly from your customers.

Why is this data so important?

Entrepreneurs are different from scientists. They don't generally want to know *why* something works; they just want to know it works. However, this is one instance where understanding the why is absolutely critical. You'll never truly realize the benefits of database marketing until you understand why customer contact information is so valuable.

It comes down to the money.

Attracting the attention of a new customer you've never dealt with before is six to seven times more expensive than reaching out to an established customer. That's a lot of money spent advertising, courting the attention of people who may or may not be interested, and attempting to lure them out of their homes, away from their computers and your competitors, and into your shop, where you then still have to sell them on your merchandise. That's a lot of work, and it takes a lot of resources.

Reaching out to established customers, on the other hand, is a bargain. You already know that these people are interested in your merchandise; no one goes to a fine apparel shop, for example, if they don't wear fine apparel. They obviously like what you've got for sale, especially if they're repeat customers. For one reason or another, there's something about your business that they like. They've come in once. You can get them again: if you're willing to do the work. If you reach out to your existing customers, and they each make one more order than they otherwise would have, you've more than doubled your investment in the relationship. You'd like an example?

Let's go to the pet food world for a moment. One thing I learned, working with a database management company—they specialize in working with customer data, identifying trends and telling me things about my customers that I might otherwise never have known—is that my customers are incredibly brand loyal. If one of my customers buys Iams dog food, they're not going to buy Purina. They're not going to buy Gravy Train. They're not even, as much as it pains me to admit it, going to buy my private label Dave's Dog Food. They're Iams customers. They're going to buy Iams.

So if I've got a special on Purina going, I'm not going to bother my Iams customers. Or if there's a buy one get one free sale on Gravy Train, or a super, super special on Dave's Dog Food, there's no sense calling these folks, or e-mailing them, or sending them a flyer. They're not going to care. They don't buy anything but Iams. This information is not relevant to them. However, if there's a fantastic deal on Iams, who do you think I'm going to call? You guessed it. I'm going to be on the phone, calling all of my Iams customers, and saying, "The food you use and your dogs love is on special now! In fact, if you come in this weekend, you'll save X amount."

My Iams shoppers will knock down the doors in response. Lest you think this is a testimonial about the brand loyalty of Iams customers, let me assure you, I could substitute Iams with any other brand name, and get the same result. It's not the product in question; it's the relevancy.

Contacting people specifically with information about sales information relevant to them is fantastically, stupendously powerful, and it's something you can only do with database marketing. You can't call all of your Iams customers, as in this example, if you don't know who your Iams customers are. You can't take advantage of the single most powerful marketing strategy mankind has ever known—giving the customer what they want—without a clear, accurate, continually updated list of who your customers are and what they want.

This concept is so powerful that you'll want to share it—in a somewhat shorter form, of course—with your crew. The better your crew understands the whys and hows of the way you do business, and what makes your store thrive, the more invested they will be in making it happen. Considering that so much of database marketing depends on your front line employees, such as cashiers and sales associates, you need them to be fully engaged in the process.

When to capture customer data

Research tells us that the beginning of the retail relationship is the most critical time. The more we see a customer during this beginning phase, the better chance we have of building a strong and more enduring relationship.

The first purchase a customer makes is often the biggest sale we'll have. It's essential to get that initial transaction into the computer. Because we know that repeated visits to our store will strengthen our relationship with the customer, we want to use that initial purchase as a building point to encourage that. The way we do this is to have our cashiers have the customer sign up, at that time, for a coupon to be used the next time they come in. That coupon has a two month time limit on it: a little time pressure to get back into the store.

Bear in mind that no matter what you do, 40 to 60 percent of the customers who come into your store one time will probably never come back. If by having your customers sign up for this coupon, you increase your return rate by 10 percent, you'll have a huge increase in business without spending any additional advertising money.

It's important to note that our cashiers are trained to say "Sign up so we can give you coupons and let you know about sales." They never, ever say "Would you like a Club Dave Card?" It's a subtle but important difference: focusing on the benefits eliminates any resistance the customer might have to sharing the information we need from them.

This is so important that we offer our cashiers an incentive to sign people up. They get five cents per enrollment, payable at the end of the month. That may not sound like much, but believe me, when the end of the month rolls around, the cashiers are all looking to see what their paycheck holds. Incentives are important. Give your crew a reason to work on your behalf—and be realistic. This is one instance in which "job security" is not enough of a reason.

What to do with that customer data

You can start using customer data right from day one. The minute you collect a piece of information about your customer, you can use it to enhance the relationship you have with that individual. You want something simple and effective? Send thank you cards.

Doing business is like dating. If you go out on a date with someone, and you have a fabulous time, do you go home and never call that person again? Do you just go about your normal daily routine, expecting that person you had so much fun with to show up out of the blue and spend more time with you? I'll tell you what: that's not going to work. Instead, if you're smart, and you want to continue your relationship with this person, you've got to take some action. You pick up the phone and call the person. You say, "Hey, that was fun! Do you want to do it again?" Maybe you don't call, but you e-mail. Or you stop by the place where that person works. The point is, you do something to let the other person know you're interested and want to keep the relationship going.

The same is true for business. If you want the relationship to grow, you need to take some action. (I know, I know, you want to hear more about the dating thing. Sorry. That's another story. If that's what you really want, you'll have to wait for Dave's Book of Dating. I'll call you when it's done.) Use your customer information to send a follow-up card. A postcard that says, "Hey, thanks for coming in the store. It was great having you here! In fact, it was so great that we want you to come back; here's a 10 percent off coupon to prove it!" or words to that effect is a powerful, effective way to give that fledgling relationship a really positive boost.

Consider your crew

I'm going to extrapolate (I know, that's a very big word for me!) a little bit from my world here. One of my stores is located in Amherst, Massachusetts, a college town if ever there was one. I joke, a little, that to work in my store there's a prerequisite that you've got to have five pounds of metal alloy in your body—in the form of earrings, eyebrow rings, nose rings, and a bunch of other rings I really don't want to think about. Why? Because that's who lives in Amherst. My crew looks like my customer base.

Mind you, if I put those same crew members in one of my other stores, they might scare some more conservative customers away. Most people are comfortable doing business with people who are like themselves. You want your customers to feel a connection with your crew, to feel that they appear to be from the same social group, even if they've never met before.

Think about it: who works the parts counter at the Harley-Davidson dealership? Chances are they've got a few tattoos, maybe a piercing or two, some black leather—the stereotypical biker image. That might not be the persona you want behind the counter at your high-end jewelry store (although you might be able to cut your security costs in half that way).

This is a really important consideration to keep in mind, especially when it comes to customer data collection. People are justifiably protective of their personal information. They've heard the same horror stories on the news that you have, and they don't want to be the victim of identity theft. You can ease a little bit of that fear by selecting crew members who resemble your customer base. People feel more comfortable sharing this type of information with people like themselves. It's another way in which the expectation has to meet the experience!

A note about customer data

Okay, so we've gone on a little bit about the beauty of database marketing and how valuable customer information is. There is one point we have to talk about. Customer information is valuable, and your customers know it's valuable.

People are worried about what you're going to do with their information. Every single night, they're exposed to news stories about identity theft and security breaches at financial institutions. Having one's personal identifying information out there can be a real headache. At a minimum, they're looking at a deluge of junk mail and spam. In the worst case scenario, they discover that a couple of teenagers in Paducah have used their social security numbers to set up ten fake credit card accounts and have ruined their credit buying video games. It can make a person a little nervous.

When you ask your customers for their personal contact information, you're asking them to trust you. It is essential that you prove yourselves worthy of that trust. How do you do that? You have to make it absolutely, positively clear—promise on your soul, your kids, your spouse, your pet—whichever one you value the most—that you'll never, ever, ever sell their information. Let your customers know that their trust in you will be well-placed. Their names, addresses, phone numbers, e-mail addresses, and other information will never, ever leave your business to benefit someone else.

And then, most critically of all, you have to honor that promise. Don't sell information. Don't trade lists. Don't spam your customers or deluge them with unwanted crap. Take the high road here. They've trusted you to do right by them when they gave over their information. Don't let them down.

Dave's Dozen

1. Know who your customers are.
2. Collect customer data to enhance your customer knowledge.
3. Don't make assumptions based on what you think you know about your customers.
4. Get out of your office and talk to your customers.
5. Cater to the customer base you want!
6. Capture customer data early in the relationship.
7. Find out if your POS system can capture customer data; if not, capture it manually.
8. Focus on benefits to get customers to sign up for loyalty cards.
9. Hire crew members who "fit" the area and type of store, so that customers will feel more comfortable.
10. Offer an incentive to your crew members to get them to sign up customers for your loyalty card program.
11. Convince customers to trust you so they'll feel comfortable sharing their personal information with you.
12. You have an obligation to protect your customer data: never, ever, ever sell or share your lists.
13. Keep in touch with your customers; you don't want them to forget about you!

Chapter 3:

Create A Great
(and Clear) Store Promise

Use your customer knowledge to create a connection

The best stores don't try to be all things to all people. That's too big a job and way too much work. It's a lot easier and a gazillion times more profitable to identify one group of customers you want to love you and focus on connecting with them.

There are a lot of ways you can connect with your customers. Think back to when we talked about Kiddlywinks. Joy Leavitt connects with her customers by demonstrating that she understands them and their children. She goes out of her way to provide the experience they're looking for. That's something we can all do. Small touches can make a big difference.

The key is to connect on an emotional level. Identify what it would take for your customers to have a great time in your store. Barnes & Noble and Borders focus on browsing opportunities for readers. Dick's Sporting Goods let you try out the gear. Every shopping excursion is the customer's opportunity to create a memory. The more memories that customers have in your store—from the great cooking class they attended to the time a crew member carried their purchases out to the car through a blinding snowstorm—the more often they'll come back.

Be of value to your customers

So now we've established that you've got to be up-front with your customers. You need to be realistic about what kind of experience they should expect from you and deliver at least that level of service. Notice I didn't say "that level of service." I said "*at least* that level of service." That's a big difference. Part of making your customers love you is doing more than the bare minimum you have to do to get by. You have to go that extra mile and provide your customers with real value.

When I talk about being of value to the customer, I like to talk about my friend Suzanne Hendery. Suzanne's got a pretty high-profile job: she's the marketing director of the Bay State Health System. The Bay State Health System is a huge organization. It includes several hospitals and God knows how many doctors, surgeons, medical professionals, administrators; you get the picture. It's a big, big outfit.

Everybody wants to do business with the Bay State Health System. That means Suzanne sees about a zillion salespeople each and every day she goes to work. Everybody and their best friend wants to sell to Suzanne. So I asked her, "What makes a great salesperson?" Her answer was simple, and it came lightning fast. Suzanne said, "The best salesperson is the one who brings me value."

She told me about one particular salesperson who does a great job with this. He sends her articles relevant to the doctors and administrators of her hospitals. Suzanne sticks a Post-it note on them, which says, "FYI—thought you might be interested! -Suzanne" and forwards them along to the appropriate parties. The result? "Everyone thinks I'm a genius!" Suzanne said. "Not only do I keep on top of my job, but I've got the time to seek out this information and pass it along to those people who value it the most." It doesn't matter what this particular salesperson is selling, Suzanne said; she has to buy from him, "because I can't live without him!"

Adding value to your customer is an extension of customer service. What do you do that no one else does? Every business has the opportunity to do that one extra thing. In our store, we carry the stuff out to our customer's cars for them. It doesn't matter if I've seen this same exact customer wrangling a one-hundred-pound bag of Corn Flakes over at the Costco. When she comes to Dave's, and she gets a case of dog food, we're going to carry it out to her car for her.

Consider the dry cleaner that stitches up a ripped seam or replaces a broken zipper. It might seem like no big deal, but to the customer, it can be a very big deal. Who's got the time to fix zippers anymore? If you sell windshield wipers, advertise that you'll put them on for people; it's a simple way to add value to your store, and it costs you nothing but a few minutes.

Adding value comes from answering the question: What can we do to make the customer's life easier? That's why, when we sell an aquarium, we're willing to come set it up for the customer. Yes, we charge for that, and no, not everybody wants the service, but for those who do, it's a real value.

Look at your business. What are the things that keep people from coming to you? What are the hassles? What are the difficulties inherent in your system? Start brainstorming ways to make life easier.

> Can your customers call orders in?
> Could your team have the order bagged and waiting for the customer, so they can stop on the way home from work and pick it up?
> Do they have to get out of their cars? Could your employees run the orders out to the parking lot?
> Do you need a drive-through window?
> What hours are you open? Could a customer have an appointment in the evenings? On the weekend?
> Could you deliver to their home? To their office? As a gift service?
> Could you offer a calendar service, reminding them of important personal dates and prompting a gift purchase? Do you offer personal shopping services?
> Can you ship merchandise for them? For their businesses?
> Could you keep the customers' credit card on file for them? Offer monthly billing?

Some of these ideas might seem off-the-wall or totally wrong for your business, but don't dismiss them all without stopping to think about them. It's doing the one little thing that no one else will do that keeps the customers coming back. Calling your customer to say "Hey, your Aunt Matilda's birthday is two weeks away!" might seem like a total waste of time—until the customer tells you to pick out a fifty-dollar gift and ship it to dear Aunt Matilda.

Let me give you another example of how you can be of value to the customer. This happened when we were getting ready to open our fourth store. The store was nowhere near ready to open yet when the salespeople started showing up. That's not surprising. It's part and parcel of doing business.

One of these salespeople was Julia. Julia was in radio sales, and I have to be honest with you. She wasn't with the best radio station. It wasn't the radio station I would have chosen to advertise on, but I didn't tell her that right off. Instead, I was honest with her, and said we weren't ready yet. There was too much to do with the new store to worry about radio advertising yet.

That didn't stop Julia. All the while we were getting the store ready, Julia would send me information. There was all this research that was relevant to the new store. How many people in the area who listened to the radio were also dog owners? How many had cats? How many raised finches? How much money did they make? How many children did they have? You get the idea. This was exactly the type of information I'd want to know. It was relevant to me, to my store, to my merchandise.

Julia provided all of this research without ever once asking for the sale. When the time came to advertise, how could I not give Julia some business? She'd done so much for me! Mind you, I still advertised with the station that would have been my first choice. Julia's services didn't erase my business sense. However, I also advertised on Julia's station, and that's something I never, ever would have done had she not made herself valuable to me.

Have absolutely unbelievable guarantees

One of the best ways to build trust with your customer and make it easy for them to do business with you is to offer absolutely unbelievable guarantees. Guarantees are great, because they remove all the risk from the transaction. If they don't like it, they can bring it back. If it doesn't work, it's free. There's nothing on the table; they're happy or it costs them nothing.

Guarantees can be a great sales tool. Consider FedEx. When you call FedEx, you don't necessarily care what it's going to cost to ship your package. You've called FedEx because they guarantee that your package is going to be there overnight. LL Bean has perhaps the best guarantee going. You open their boxes and find "Guaranteed. Period." They send a return authorization in with the package. They practically send a postman to wait for you to send the merchandise back. If they made it any easier to return things, they'd have to camp out on your front door. As a result, people feel very, very confident doing business with LL Bean. There's no risk.

Our guarantee is funny: If your dog won't eat Dave's Dog Food, I will. The realistic part of the guarantee is the 100 percent money back portion; no one's shown up yet with a bowlful and a fork, but that's because our food is so good.

So what makes a great guarantee? A guarantee has two parts: the condition and the promise. The condition is the "if" part: If your dog won't eat the dog food, if you don't like the merchandise, if it doesn't fit, if it doesn't work, or so on. The promise is the payoff: what you will do if the condition applies. Will you eat the dog food, take the merchandise back, return the money, fix the problem? Think through your guarantees; they have to be simple, concise, and believable. Never make a promise that you're not willing to keep.

For example, we guarantee all of the parakeets we sell for life. What does that mean, you ask? That's the same question our customers ask, and here's what we tell them: we'll guarantee this parakeet forever. It could be for fifty years, and parakeets only live, on average, fifteen to twenty years. If it dies, we'll replace it, for free—provided you buy your parakeet care supplies and food from us. We can verify this information, because we track all purchases in our database. With that information, we know you're taking adequate care of the parakeet, and if you're taking good care of the birds, we'll take care of you.

Of course, due to the nature of our business, we reserve the right not to honor that guarantee if we believe that someone is abusing the parakeets. Every retailer's going to have those products or situations that require specific guarantees. In those cases, you have to know *exactly* what you're guaranteeing. Be really, really explicit with your guarantee. This is one area where there are no shades of gray—it all has to be black and white.

You have to train your employees to honor the guarantee. This is a natural extension of the customer service mind-set: your crew has to treat the customer the way they want to be treated. Ask them how they like to be treated when they return something to the store. They have to know not to give anyone any grief during the returns process: if they do, they destroy the integrity of the guarantee. If you've got an employee who just doesn't get it, you need to get rid of that person. It's that important: The trust your customers have in you rises and falls on the way you honor your guarantee.

Every business should have something that it guarantees. Many times, we don't realize what we do that we could guarantee; there might be part of our everyday business that we totally take for granted, yet it could easily form the basis for a guarantee.

For example: if you're a dry cleaner, you could guarantee that if a button gets broken during the cleaning process, you'll replace it, free of charge, with a matching button. Now, this might be something you'd do ordinarily without thinking about it. Chances are you'd perform this service for no charge. But to guarantee it—to make a promise that you'll do this, no matter what, and honor that promise—can serve as a way to set your dry cleaning business apart from every other dry cleaner in town. I'll tell you what: I'm a fussy guy, when it comes to my clothes. If a dry cleaner guaranteed that there'd be no wrinkles in my shirt collar, I'd give my business to that dry cleaner without thinking twice.

H&R Block has helped secure their hold on the tax preparation market, a market that's being chipped away by do-it-yourself-software, by their guarantee. If the IRS wants to audit you, H&R Block will be right there beside you. That's a very tangible way of removing risk for the customer, and it has helped drive customers away from the software shelves and into the office.

Think about guarantees when selecting your merchandise. Beyond what guarantees you as a retailer can offer, there are also manufacturer's guarantees. We carry one particular brand of bird feeders (Droll Yankee Bird Feeders) that offers a lifetime guarantee. It's a line that's not carried in the chain stores, yet it practically sells itself because the product is fully guaranteed. A crazy squirrel cracks the plastic or an overly plump pigeon takes out a perch, just bring it in; we'll give you another one, free of charge. When you offer unconditional guarantees like that, it removes all the risk for your customers.

Be the expert

If your customers are going to trust you, it helps if they think you know what you're talking about. How are they going to know if you know your stuff? One way is to get out into the community and show them. Become the local authority on weddings or the bird watching pro. Develop a reputation as the Answer Man (or Woman). Speak to clubs about your passion and your business. There are literally dozens of ways to establish your position as an expert in a given area. People like to do business with the best; if you can demonstrate that you're the most knowledgeable source on a given subject, they're going to come to you.

That's the concept behind Shield Sports. When Shield Sports opens a new store, they select who they're going to hire and then send them to other, existing stores for up to three to four months' worth of training. They want to ensure that everyone on their team is an absolute expert on athletic equipment and gear, and people go to Shield Sports for that expertise.

Some ways to demonstrate your expertise include:

> writing articles or columns for the local newspaper;
> creating or contributing to a blog;
> appearing on TV (I do this one; I've had my own half hour TV show (Dave's Pet Show) since 1995.);
> being a guest on radio call-in programs;
> speaking to local clubs;
> and hosting classes, seminars, or events at your store.(Here's a little secret if you do that last one: Rotary Club, Kiwanis, and other local business-theme club audiences absolutely love hearing how you got started in business and how you compete with the big guys. Inside every listener beats the heart of a would-be entrepreneur. Ninety-nine percent of them will never do anything about it, but that doesn't mean they're not curious!)

If you've got it, flaunt it

If you have great guarantees and expertise, you have to communicate that to the customer. If you consistently offer great customer service, let the public know. Make this a cornerstone of your store's personality. Put it out there: when you come to Dave's, you're going to be treated better than you would be anywhere else. Many businesses do things for customers and never once consider the marketing opportunities therein. The plumber who always cleans up after every job, the laundromat that does repairs, the skate sharpener that will put new laces in your skates every visit—all of these businesses could have a real competitive advantage if they told customers and potential customers about the specific ways they're different from their competition.

Don't ever say "We offer great customer service" and leave it at that. Be specific. By saying "If a button comes off, we guarantee to replace it with a matching button," you're effectively communicating an attention to detail and genuine concern about the customer. That's customer service. Don't say those words unless you can own them, but if you can own them, you'd better say them!

Advantages of being a small business

A lot of retailers use the fact that they're the local, hometown alternative as part of their appeal. That can be a great idea; after all, it's one definite way to differentiate yourself from the big chain retailers. If you've got it, flaunt it, right?

The flip side of this is that if you're going to position yourself as the local, hometown alternative, you've got to deliver local, hometown service. Remember: people like to do business with the little guy, but they have big expectations of the small retailer. Not only do you have to have better service, better merchandise, and better product knowledge than the big guys, you need to treat each and every customer like a good neighbor. If you can do this, great! It's a fabulous way to position yourself. But don't ever think being the local guy gives you a free pass.

Dave's Dozen

1. Don't be afraid to be yourself!
2. Don't try to be all things to all people; be who you are.
3. Small actions can do a lot to make customers feel like they're in "their" type of place.
4. Invest time in your customers; it will pay off big time.
5. Have the strongest, clearest, most dependable guarantee of anyone in your industry, and certainly in your marketplace.

6. Seek out manufacturers who have particularly strong guarantees: this enhances your own store guarantees.

7. How your crew honors your guarantee determines the success of your business.

8. Don't promise more than you can deliver.

9. Understand what your customer finds important. That's what you need to provide to be of value.

10. Being of value means going the extra mile and doing that thing no one else does.

11. Every retailer has an opportunity to be of value.

12. Be the expert. Demonstrating your knowledge is a great way to earn the customer's trust.

13. Train your crew to be experts, too!

Chapter 4:

Make Sure You Deliver on the Promise

The experience and the expectations have to match

The experience your customers have in your store has to match the expectation they came to you with. Expectations come from a lot of places: your advertising, your reputation, the way you conduct yourself. As long as these expectations match what your customers find when they set foot in your place, you're all right.

The problems kick in when you've got a disconnect between the marketing and the reality. If you promise your customers that they'll be treated like a fairy-tale princess but your crew treats them like Cinderella's ugly cousin Beulah, you've got a problem. If you tell people you have the latest, greatest merchandise, straight off the boat from Europe's hottest designers, and they come in to discover nothing that they couldn't find at the discount store, you've let your customers down. If you tell the world that you're the world's expert on fly-fishing but you can't tell the difference between a shark and a sardine, you're not going to last long.

Promise anything—as long as you can keep that promise. Your advertisements are a kind of promise: everything in there should be something you can back up. If you go on the radio and say "Come to Bert's for the Best Beads!" you'd better have the best beads.

Be honest. There's nothing wrong with being a bare-bones store that focuses on good value and friendly service; it's certainly worked for Costco! Own who you are. Be proud of your business, and represent yourself accurately. That way, the expectations your customers come to you with will match the experience they have.

Of course, there's nothing wrong with surpassing expectations. Costco focuses on low prices and large sizes, but they also have friendly, knowledgeable staffers. A great example of this, from the independent retail world, occurred at a place called Master's Jewelers. Now, you probably don't know this, but I've got a wife and a daughter. They both like me at the moment, and to keep it that way, I make sure to buy them jewelry every now and then. Master's is owned by a local guy, just like me, and I like doing business with him. Over the years, I've spent a fair amount at Master's.

I bought my wife Ellen a watch. We didn't get it from Master's, because they didn't carry the brand she had her heart set on. But when we got the watch, it was too large for Ellen's wrist. She took it down to Fred, the jeweler at Master's, to see if they could remove a link from the strap and make it fit better. I trusted his expertise and knew he could do a good job for us. Fred worked on Ellen's watch for hours to get the link out so it would fit her properly. It turned out to be unexpectedly difficult, but at the end of the day, how much do you think the folks at Master's charged Ellen for their time?

Not a dime. Now I never expected that. I'd assumed Fred would charge us, and I happily would have paid it. After all, his time and expertise is valuable. When I went back in to thank him, Fred simply smiled. It was no big deal, he assured me. Just something they do for their customers.

That's when the reality can surpass the expectation. That's how the independent retailer can totally wow even the toughest critic, and believe me, I can be a tough critic! Oh, by the way, that free labor to get the link out ended up "costing" me a pair of earrings for my daughter Alison and a bracelet for Ellen! Talk about smart business.

I'm sure there are things you can do to take care of your good customers. Just like Fred knew that this type of attention pays off in the end, the same will hold true in your business. That's why we'll always clip birds' wings for the owners. That's why other retailers offer free gift wrapping, or the tailor touts free alterations for life: that little bit of extra attention can be the one thing that makes your customer love you.

Think things through

If you're going to be of value to your customers, you really need to think through the way you operate every aspect of your business. Let me give you an example: My wife and I use a specific dry cleaner, and we go there a lot. I mean a lot! Every single week we've got thirty to forty dollars worth of dry cleaning. That's a lot of suit jackets and dresses.

This particular dry cleaner runs an ad campaign, in which coupons are printed on the back of the receipt at local grocery stores. The coupon's good for 10 percent off your dry cleaning bill. Needless to say, we use these coupons regularly.

But I stopped at the dry cleaner one day, and I didn't have the coupon. The owner wouldn't give me the 10 percent off, despite the fact that I was in there every single week, doing a tremendous amount of business with them. I was not a happy camper. I took the cleaning and left, telling the clerk he'd never see me again. For the sake of four or five dollars, they lost thousands of dollars worth of business.

Think it through. If you're going to offer value to your customers, especially your best customers, you can't get tied up in bureaucratic BS! Whether I had the coupon or not was immaterial: the fact is I was in there every single week, doing lots of business. The 10 percent off was the value, and withholding the value lost them 100 percent of the business.

The Outback story

Let me give you an example of how the failure to think things through can be a real headache.

Every now and then, my wife Ellen and I go out for dinner at the local Outback Steakhouse. It's a good place to eat, but there's one issue with it: the light fixtures over the tables just hang too low. If you're a tall guy like me, you're going to knock your head against them, unless you're really careful. The light fixtures over the booths, however, are higher. I can sit there without hitting my head, no problem.

When Ellen and I arrived at the restaurant one evening, it was clear that things were pretty slow. There weren't a lot of cars in the parking lot. Stepping inside, we saw lots of empty tables and booths. This was pretty good news, at least for me—I'm sure the local Outback manager wasn't so thrilled about it!—and I asked the hostess if we could be seated in a booth.

Her answer shocked me: "No." There were clearly lots of empty booths and tables, so I asked her why. "If you sit over there, I won't have a server to wait on you." "I suggest you find one," I told her, "because that's where we're sitting." She found a server, of course, but that's not the point. When I talked to the manager the next morning, he was astonished by his hostess's reaction to my seating request. "That's not how we do things," he assured me. But you know what? If that's the experience that my wife and I, and other customers, are having, that is how you do business. The expectation and the experience were completely out of alignment, and unless that manager worked immediately to change the situation, he was going to have real trouble on his hands, and soon.

Every experience like the one I just told you about wrecks your brand. Every single person who works for you, from the hostess seating guests to the advisor fielding questions to the order taker answering the phones to the cashier ringing up the order has a direct, immediate, and overwhelming effect on your brand. No matter how successfully you've built your brand up, it can be destroyed, immediately, by the actions of one crew member. Your team's ability to deliver products and services in the expected fashion can build your brand up or tear it down.

That's why it's essential that you don't promise what you can't deliver. If you advertise that you have great customer service, and the customer shows up to discover that the sales crew is far more interested in discussing last night's football game than helping them, your brand is diminished. If you market yourself as expert advisors, when a customer calls with a problem regarding her account, and she's funneled through a voice mail maze only to be greeted with a "Well, I don't know the answer to that question," your brand is damaged.

Remember, your brand is not what you think it is. It is what the customer thinks it is. Your customer's thinking is affected by two elements here: the advertising and the experience. They have to match or be even better than expected. It's a matter of trust.

The importance of trust

The title of this book says it all: Make your customers love you. How do you do that? A really big component of it comes down to trust. Your customers have to be willing to trust you before you can really develop a relationship with them.

This really came home to me during the spring of 2007, the time of the pet food recalls. Even if you're not in the pet food industry, chances are you heard about or were affected by the massive pet food recall. Tainted pet food caused the death of numerous animals, and the public was thrown into a panic. That's when the value of trust became clear to me. In fact, this story is the crux of why we're still in business today, and why we're growing and thriving in a world where independent retailers have a hard time of it.

When the pet food recall hit, our business was in a pretty good position. We'd been operating for thirty-two years at that point. We had a good customer base, strong and steady. That didn't mean we had the business of everyone in town; in fact, it was quite the opposite. Over the years, we'd spent a fortune on advertising, and still there were people who would never, ever set foot in our store. They didn't come in, because they didn't need us. They were happy with what they were buying, and where they were buying it.

Then the recall hit. Pets were dying, there was a confusing cloud of misinformation out there, and people just didn't know what to do. That's when we ran one simple ad. It read: "If you are frightened or even confused about what to feed your pet, come to Dave's."

That ad appealed directly to the customer's concerns, and reinforced the fact that we knew what we were talking about and could be trusted. It was at this point that all the time, energy, and effort that went into building the Dave's brand paid off. People who had never had a reason to visit us before had one now; they were afraid, and they needed the advice of someone they could trust. That someone was us, and we communicated that fact with our ad. It drew in the business in a way no ad has ever done for us before or since.

Our private label dog food had been in existence for fifteen years at that point. It was absolutely at that moment, during the pet food recall, that demand for it exploded. It's insane how much Dave's Pet Food we sold at that point. Why? Because the customer knew they could trust us, even if they'd never shopped with us before.

Trust is especially important if you offer services. How many times have you taken your car to the mechanic because it was making some god-awful noise under the hood? You're sure it's going to cost hundreds and hundreds of dollars to fix it, but your mechanic reaches under there, fiddles around for a few minutes, fixes the problem, and sends you on your way. He may charge you, he may not, but what he doesn't do is create an expensive way to fix what was obviously a simple problem.

There are times when saying "You don't need this right now" is the absolute best thing you can do for your customers. They appreciate not only your honesty, but the fact that you're forgoing what could be a very profitable sale at their expense. Customers aren't stupid: they know you're in business to make money. What they don't like is when you take advantage of that. When you demonstrate that you're not taking advantage, you earn their trust.

In fact, we're putting together an ad campaign right now telling people not to buy something. You see, a few weeks ago, I got a letter from a customer, detailing why we shouldn't sell rabbits, all the horrible things that happen to rabbits when they go into a home that's not prepared for a bunny, and more. I did some research, and while we're still going to sell rabbits, concerns for the health and safety of our animals has been and will always be of paramount importance at

Dave's. That's why we're launching the "Please don't buy a bunny for Easter!" ad campaign. We want customers who buy a rabbit to be well-informed and prepared about their purchase. The signs we're hanging include the facts about what's required to keep a bunny happy and healthy; if those facts scare someone away from buying a rabbit, that's okay. Both parties will probably be better off that way. Will it cost me a few sales? Sure, but that cost is more than outweighed by the value of the trust my customers will gain in me as a retailer who truly walks the walk and cares about his animals.

I don't know what industry you're in, but there are parallels in any number of fields, from the jeweler who pays special attention to the backgrounds of the diamonds he sells to the apparel retailer who refuses to deal with manufacturers who run sweatshops. Every industry has a line in the sand; you want your customers to know you're on the right side of that line.

Don't lie to your customers

If I have one pet peeve, it's businesses lying to their customers. Being honest is good business. Yet I see people lying to their customers all of the time. They do this, thinking it's an easy way to make a quick buck. It might mean quick money once, but it'll mean less money in the long run. People want to do business with—and they spend more money with—people they like and trust. You cannot trust someone who lies to you.

Think about it this way: if you had a vendor who promised you one thing and delivered another, how long would you buy from him? If a salesperson told you your order would be there in two days, and it took two months, would you order from her again? I'm guessing the answer's a big no because you're like me. You don't like to be lied to.

Guess what. Your customers don't like it either. Here's an example for you. The current rage in my industry, spurred in part by the massive pet food recalls a few years ago now, is for organic pet food. People want to know that the food they're giving their pets is safe. That's why they're seeking out the all-natural, organic, quality food.

There's a huge market for it. It's a lucrative product. Our high end, private label all natural organic dog food sells for thirty-six dollars. There's another product out there called Timberwolf Organics that charges sixty dollars for the same-sized bag. But Timberwolf Organics isn't organic at all. Due to some legal loopholes, they can't be sued. They're not technically breaking any laws.

What they are doing, technically or otherwise, is lying to the customer. Anyone looking at that bag and reading that name is going to think the contents of that dog food bag are organic. Guess how they feel when they discover it's not organic. Guess how they feel when they discover that after paying sixty dollars for it. If you guessed really, really unhappy, you're pretty darn close to the answer. If you guessed absolutely furious, you're even closer.

When customers ask me why they should pay more for that given product, I say, "I can't give you an honest answer. It beats me!" I don't say this to steer them toward my private label product; there are other organic pet foods out there that are a great value, and are honest with the consumer. I'll help the customer find whatever is best for that customer and their dogs. It's about the value, and more importantly, the honesty. I'd rather have my customers trust me and never sell them one bag of my private label. People trust me and they trust my crew. I plan to keep it that way.

If you lie to your customers, it will always come back to bite you in the butt. That's not poetry, but it's true. Remember this: brands come and go, and vendors may not always toe the most ethical line, but your store must be above reproach. Your customers have to know that they can trust you.

Trust is an obligation

Trust is wonderful. Trust is great. Trust is the best thing you can have. Trust is what you can use to build a fantastic relationship with your customers.

But trust isn't free; it's an obligation. When your customers trust you, you owe them something.

Here's another example from the days of the pet food recall. I got a phone call then that really opened my eyes. (Boy, those of you who are reading the book to see how I screw up on a daily basis are going to love this story. You should pay me double, just for all the laughs you're getting!)

So, anyway, I'm in my office, calm and Zen-like as usual, with faxed copies of the latest recall list piling up on my desk and papers flying in every direction, when the phone rings. It's an irate customer, and she wants to talk to me. "How come," she demanded, "you call me each and every time Iams goes on sale, but you can't pick up your phone and tell me if the dog food I'm giving my dogs is safe or not?" I swallowed. There was only one answer to this question, if I was going to be honest with this customer. "Because I'm a nitwit," I told her. "And as soon as I get off the phone with you, we're going to start doing exactly that." She was right. If our customers were going to continue to trust us, they needed to be able to lean on us in this, a time of real need. We spent the next days and weeks calling and e-mailing the affected customers every time the recall list was adjusted. We also let the customers who used Dave's Pet Food know it was safe and not affected by the recall. It was important to our customers to know that the food they were feeding their dogs was safe, and it became our role to let them know.

That's the price of trust, and believe me, it's totally worth it.

Trust is for the dogs

For years and years and years, customers would ask me, "When are you going to start selling puppies?"

People love dogs. Heck, I love dogs. Dogs are the whole reason this business is where it is today. There was obviously a demand for dogs, and so one day, when the drugs had kicked in, I decided it was time to go into the puppy business. I called the state authorities and said, "Hey, I'm thinking of selling puppies. What should I know?"

They were thrilled that I called, (usually retailers wait until after they've started the business to find out exactly what they're supposed to do) and gave me all kinds of information about the ideal set up, and how to care for the dogs, and what the best way to handle puppies was.

They recommended, to minimize disease and contagion, that dogs be kept individually in small cages. Now, I don't know about you, but I just couldn't do that. It breaks my heart to see all those sad dogs in small cages. If we were going to sell puppies, we were going to have happy puppies. So we built 10'x10' pens for the puppies so that they could play together and socialize. In short, we made sure that their time with us was going to be happy and healthy.

Then I went to suppliers, and I made sure that we were only dealing with reputable breeders. The type of breeders who could face an investigative crew from *60 Minutes* with a smile and a happy hello—no puppy mills for Dave's!

We put up signs recommending that people visit animal shelters to adopt dogs. We put up signs saying our puppies were guaranteed for life, and that we would always take the dogs back; we didn't want any abandoned dogs, or dogs dropped off at shelters, because the owners couldn't deal with them. And that's it; we were in the puppy business.

Sales exploded. It was absolutely unbelievable how many puppies we sold. We sold more puppies than I'd ever imagined possible, and I have a great imagination; I can imagine a lot of sales.

Then the phone call came. The owner of the second puppy we'd ever sold, a beautiful golden retriever, discovered that the puppy had a hip problem and needed major surgery. Five thousand dollars' worth of major surgery, in fact.

For a moment, I wondered why we'd gone into the puppy business. It was at this point that I took my own advice and asked the customer how we could fix the problem. I was fully prepared to pay the five thousand dollars, but it turns out she had insurance on the dog and only wanted us to help pay for the portion of surgery not covered by insurance. Of course I agreed. We'd guaranteed the puppies, and our reputation was on the line.

The customer came down while I was writing the check. She was amazed that there was no problem and that I was willing to just write the check on the spot. While she was waiting, she looked around the store, and saw something she liked. She got out her cell phone, and called a friend: "You've got to get down here! They've got the most adorable Yorkie, and he's only twelve hundred dollars!" That's the power of trust. She'd bought a dog from us, had a problem, trusted us to fix the problem, and in the midst of having the problem fixed, felt confident enough in us and our word to recommend that her friend come purchase another puppy from us.

Dave's Dozen

1. Your customers have to trust you before you can have a relationship with them.
2. Concentrate on making your customers feel safe doing business with you.
3. Creating trust takes action; it's more than the words.
4. Make sure to deliver at least the level of customer service you promise.
5. Guarantees, policies, and the way you resolve problems all help create trust.
6. Failing to deliver on a promise is the fastest way to destroy trust.
7. Don't let bureaucracy kill customer service!
8. Consider every aspect of your business; do they match all the promises you've made?
9. Being honest is good business.
10. Be willing to take a stand on your customers' behalf.
11. Don't lie to your customers, even to support a vendor's claims.

12. Customers aren't stupid; you're not going to be able to trick them.
13. Trust is an obligation: you have to be on the lookout for your customers.

Chapter 5:

Have a Customer-first Attitude

New customers are great. There's almost nothing better than seeing someone come into your store for the first time, a big smile on their face, and then watching them leave with bulging bags. If that customer tells his family and friends what a great store you have and how much fun it is to shop there, that's even better. You can't have a great, growing business without new customers. But while you're working on attracting new customers, you've also got to focus on making your current customers come back, especially after they've had a bad experience. It's going to happen: mistakes get made, crew members screw up, merchandise breaks. When bad stuff happens, it's up to you to transform an upset, unhappy customer into a satisfied, loyal one.

Abandoning the last word

If you want the customer to come back, you and your crew have to do something really, really difficult. You have to abandon the last word.

Abandoning the last word is the essence of customer service. When you truly understand customer service—when you "get it"—you realize that the transaction is about the customers and their needs. It's not about you. If you have a person who can't do that, who absolutely can't abandon the need to be right, no matter what, you need to get rid of him. If you are that person, get some help.

You see, at the end of the day, it doesn't matter how much you know. No one cares if you're the most knowledgeable electronics guru on the West Coast or the top wine expert in the entire world. You're not trying out for the debate team. You have to shut up and listen. What customers care about is that you've listened to them, you've heard what they had to say, and you did your level best to make them happy.

That's hard to swallow sometimes, I know. This is particularly true for those of you in the professional services field. There will be clients who absolutely insist on making the totally wrong decision for themselves, no matter what you tell them. Of course you want to offer the wiser alternatives, but there comes a time in every conversation when you have to let it go.

Here's the suggestion I give to my own employees. When a situation arises and you've got an unhappy customer, simply say, "I'm sorry there was a screwup; what would you like me to do to fix it?" (This is an almost magical sentence, which I'll be discussing more later on.) I'll tell you what, ninety-nine times out of a hundred, this simple sentence defuses the entire situation. You can practically see everyone's blood pressure going down. You might even feel your own blood pressure going down. You haven't admitted you were wrong—-you might have been, and you and I both know you might not have been, but that's not the point—you've moved past that issue into resolving the problem.

Customers love that, and it's incredibly powerful. Give it a try, and see what happens. In fact, when you do try it, shoot me an e-mail at Dave@DaveRatner.com and let me know how it worked. Maybe you'll wind up in the next book!

Of course, like everything else I've learned in life, part of this philosophy came out of a mistake. Let me tell you about it. I call this my "George and the Turtle" story.

George and the turtle

In one of my stores, my fish and reptile departments were just not what they could be. It was kind of a dismal situation: we were losing fish, the snakes were sluggish, and things just didn't look good. No one was buying, because things weren't fabulous: fish and reptiles are very visual products. If they don't look good, they don't sell.

Then we hired George. It was as if a miracle had occurred, right there in my reptile department. The tanks were sparkling, the fish were swimming in formation, the turtles were tap-dancing—you get the picture? Things were fabulous. George transformed our fish and reptile department.

Then one day, in came a six-year-old boy. His parents were with him, walking with somber expressions on their faces. The kid was crying, tears running down his face. And he was clutching a crumpled, brown paper bag. He walked through my store to this shiny, brilliant, stunning fish and reptile department. He handed the bag, almost reverently, to George, and told him, "My turtle died."

George took the bag and opened it. He carefully examined the turtle, looking at its shell, the tiny, closed eyes, the wrinkled ends of reptilian legs. Then he pronounced his wisdom: "Yup. You killed it."

Just to put the icing on the cake, he tossed the bag, turtle and all, into the trash, right in front of the kid.

The parents were furious. They were headed right through the roof, and who can blame them? Right in front of them, their child was heartbroken, and my employee had just made it ten times worse. Luckily, I was in the store. I hustled over and got George out of there on the double. I calmed the parents down and brought over my very best kid-friendly sales guy. We got the kid set up with another turtle, a turtle tank, turtle food—the whole bit.

After he went home, we called that kid every hour, on the hour, for a week, to make sure the turtle was okay. I lost sleep worrying about that turtle. Making sure that turtle was happy and healthy became an obsession.

Luck was with us. The new turtle was fine, and the kid was thrilled. He wrote us a great letter, thanking us for taking so much time with him and helping him get his new turtle settled in. We even wound up including the kid on one of our television commercials.

What about George, you ask? I fired him. He didn't understand it. He had no clue why he didn't have a job with us anymore because he was right. The kid had killed the turtle, or rather, his mother had, when she washed out the turtle bowl with Clorox. In George's mind, that was the most important thing. But it wasn't. Making that little boy—that teeny, tiny, heartbroken customer, clutching that brown paper bag—happy again was the most important thing. George just did not get that. He absolutely could not see it. In his mind, if was far more important for him to be right.

And that's fine—as long as he's right in someone else's store. When you're on your own time, you can hog the last word all you want. If you want to be flat-out obnoxious, insisting that you're right, no matter what, be my guest. Of course, I won't be in a hurry to get myself invited to your dinner parties, but that's not the issue here. When you're in the store, when you're on the sales floor, when you're working one-on-one with that client, you've got to surrender the power of the last word. It's not the most important thing in the world to be right all of the time. Let it go. Concentrate on what's really at issue here: making the customers so happy that they'll want to come back.

Dave's Dozen

1. Abandon the last word!
2. Remember, it's more important that the customer's happy than that you're right.
3. Deep down, the customer doesn't care who's right and who's wrong: they just know that there's a problem and they want it fixed *fast*!
4. You can resolve problems without admitting you're wrong.
5. Say "I'm sorry there was a screwup. How would you like me to fix it?"
6. Allowing the customer to dictate how to fix the problem is the best thing you can do!

7. Try to see the problem from the customer's point of view; it will make resolving the issue easier.

8. Customers will love you for resolving the issue.

9. Remember that an employee can be technically brilliant and completely incapable of abandoning the last word—look at George!

10. If you have an employee who can't grasp this concept, get rid of him or her.

11. If you can't grasp this concept, get help.

12. It's never too late to attempt to fix a problem.

13. Let me know how this strategy works for you by e-mailing me at Dave@DaveRatner.com.

Chapter 6:

Have a Clear "Damage Control" Policy

I'm going to start this bit out with a little bit of news. Every single person reading this book will make a mistake. Your employees will make mistakes. Everyone makes mistakes. No one is perfect, and that includes me. In fact, the only thing I may be perfect at is making mistakes. The minute I'm done with this book, I might just start a book detailing all the mistakes I've ever made. Of course, I'm not sure I can afford all the paper it will take to write them down, but I'll worry about that when I get there.

So let's take the fact that mistakes are going to happen as a given. Things will go wrong. People will screw up. Your crew members will say the wrong thing, or they'll say the right thing, but the customer will take it the wrong way. Merchandise won't arrive when it's supposed to, special orders won't fit, and the best-thing-since-sliced-bread product everyone wants will sell out so fast that you've got crowds of disappointed shoppers.

The question is: what are you going to do about it? The answer to that question can be found in your damage control policy.

The importance of having a damage control policy

You have to have a damage control policy. You can't just wing it. You need a way to handle disappointed, angry customers and to fix mistakes. Here's a little secret: customers will forgive almost anything if you address the problem right away and take action to make it better. Ninety-nine out of a hundred people are blown away when a business owner actively seeks to fix a problem; so many customers are used to having their concerns totally ignored!

There are two types of problems that can occur in your business: things that are within your control and things that are totally out of your hands. It might be your fault that no one ordered Super Product Number Four that week. On the other hand, the Super Product factory might have burned to the ground, and no one in the whole nation has any Super Products. The customer's not going to care either way. It doesn't matter one bit to them whether it's a problem in your stockroom or Stockholm; they want what they want, and they want it now. I'm guessing this is not an unfamiliar scenario to you.

Don't waste any time discussing the reasons behind a problem with your customer. Realize that it doesn't matter why something went wrong, or who's at fault. The customers don't care. They just know that there's a problem, and they want it fixed.

Let the customer define the fix

Here's what you need to do. If you can master this, you'll have more than gotten your money's worth out of this book. Remember the magical sentence I mentioned on page seventy-one? Well, this one little sentence will save you thousands of dollars, help you keep your customers, and keep your customers happy. You want to read and re-read this sentence until it's burned into your memory. You want all of your employees to know this sentence the way they know their phone numbers. You should have this sentence permanently engraved in your consciousness and tattooed on the forearms of your cashiers.

Okay, maybe not that last bit. Not unless they're really into tattoos. Here's the essential damage control policy-related sentence you need to know: **I'm sorry there was a screwup; what would you like me to do to fix it?** The words are simple enough, but they're also the most powerful, best way to remedy a mistake. There's no explaining. You don't try to weasel out of the situation or shift the blame someplace else. It's short and to the point: you acknowledge that there is a problem and start the process of repairing it in a few short words. Customers respond well to this. Most people don't actually want you to do anything about the situation. They just want you to know there was a problem. The most important thing is that you heard their concern and took it seriously.

If they do want you to do something, it'll be far less than what you'd offer on your own. Often, it's a simple repair of the immediate situation: exchanging a broken item for a fixed one, or honoring the sale price for the merchandise they were charged full price for. If it's beyond that, it's still often less than you might have spontaneously offered. Yet you know that this is what the customer wants in order to be happy; after all, it was her idea!

Here's an example: We've got four pretty good stores, but we do make mistakes. (Just wanted to put that out there in case you were thinking we're perfect.) One of the mistakes had to do with our voice mail: for some reason, it stated we were open until five o'clock, even though one of our stores closed at four o'clock.

One day, a customer called and got the voice mail that said we were open until five. She drove down to our store, a ten mile trip, to get some dog biscuits. When she arrived at four thirty, the store was closed. You can imagine the voice mail message waiting for me! She was hysterically angry, and who could blame her?

I called her, and said, "You must be furious! I'd be livid, if that happened to me." Hearing me say that calmed her down. I assured her that we'd fix the voice mail, which is the solution she wanted to the problem. Then I said we'd ship her a box of biscuits, and throw in a five-dollar gift certificate for her trouble.

This absolutely shocked her. Never in a million years had she imagined that her phone call would result in a free box of biscuits—delivered to her home, no less, and with a gift certificate as well. Had we done nothing, this customer would have told her friends what jerks we were, and how we were so stupid we couldn't even get our own voice mail right. Instead, now she'll tell them how fabulous we are, and how we really care about the customer.

And that we fixed the voice mail, which we did, right away!

Another customer e-mailed me, concerned about the state of the birds in one of our stores. I thanked her, checked out the situation myself, and made sure what needed fixing got fixed. You'd better believe she noticed. She e-mailed me back after the bird section was in better shape. Not only was she thrilled with the improvements we had made, she'd bought another cockatiel from us!

Empower employees to fix problems

You're not going to be on the spot to take care of each problem that arises. Therefore, you have to give your employees the freedom to fix problems. When you've got a good crew, a team that understands that its number one priority is to convince the customer to come back, you've got a great thing. You don't want to hamstring their effectiveness by forcing them to check with management every time they're attempting to solve an issue.

Trust your team. If they know that giving that angry customer a free bag of dog food is going to turn the situation around, let them give away the dog food. Owners often hold on to control and attempt to micromanage customer service for fear of their employees "giving away the store," and I'll tell you what: in all the years I've been doing this, I've never once had an employee give away too much. Please don't worry that your crew will go overboard. It just doesn't happen.

In fact, you should be more worried about the opposite. If you're anything like me, and your crew's anything like mine, they'll be overcautious. When my crew does make a mistake, nine times out of ten, it's because they're erring on the side of caution. They want to protect the store, and it makes them timid. You can't blame them: they've got your best interests at heart. You just need to provide the support, training, and culture so they understand that your best interest is to make the customer happy and keep them that way!

Here we've stolen a page from Stew Leonard's, the grocery chain famous around the world for their customer service. At Stew Leonard's, the motto is:

Rule #1: The customer is always right.

Rule #2: If the customer is ever wrong, re-read rule #1.

Our employees are told: If you ever think you have to tell a customer no, talk to a manager! This gives them the freedom to err on the side of generosity. If they're not sure what to do, they can go to management. All of the managers in our stores are told that unless the customer is really, really abusive, they are empowered to do whatever it takes to solve the problem.

My managers know that I'm going to be okay with whatever they decide, as long as the customer leaves happy. The only way I'm going to flip out about a decision my manager makes at this point is if the customer is still unhappy, and the problem hasn't been resolved!

Call your customers

An essential part of damage control is calling your customers to head off problems. There's going to come a time in your business when you absolutely, positively have to do this. Stuff happens: orders don't arrive, employees screw up, one of your crew members has a psychotic break and acts in such an offensive manner you don't even know what to say about it. There's a big problem, your customer is really unhappy, and you need to do something.

This is when you pick up the phone and give that customer a call. I'm going to tell you something: When the owner of a business calls a customer, it absolutely blows that customer away. He's flabbergasted. No one, but no one, expects the owner of the store to call them to fix a problem. However, part of fixing a problem is reaching out to the customer, and sometimes that means a phone call. Before you call the customer, make sure you're:

Calm (This may require Jack Daniels, Quaaludes, or other tranquilizers of your choosing!)

> Ready to listen to the customer
> Prepared with at least some version of the problem
> Prepared to fix the problem

And, of course, when you make the call, be ready with the magic sentence: **I'm sorry there was a screwup; what would you like me to do to fix it?** More often than not, there's not anything the customer wants you to do. She wants you to be aware that there is a problem, and to hear her concerns, and that's it. Some customers will want something—a replacement for a broken item, a free meal—but even then, they'll usually ask for less than you would have spontaneously offered them in an effort to resolve the issue.

This raises a really good point. Calling your customers gives you more than the chance to fix the problem. It also offers the chance to get a real insight into how things are really going in your business. Customers are not shy; if you ask their honest opinion, they're going to give it to you.

Mind you, they're floored when you first call them, but that wears off. Once they know you want to hear what's really happening, they're going to let you have it. It's far easier for them to tell you this information over the phone; most people would never dream of saying this stuff face-to-face. A lot of times you'll hear "I love your place, but—" Those buts are pure gold. You want the buts. The buts are what you need to know about. This is information you can't get any other way.

And when you hear about something negative in one of these conversations, you absolutely, positively have to act on it. Not only does this show that you listen to your customers, which will make them love you, but it reinforces and strengthens their involvement with and relationship to your store.

What a damage control policy can do for you

There are lots of things a good damage control policy can do for you. The short version is this: you'll have fewer headaches, and you'll make more money. Here's the long version, looking at the three things a damage control policy can do for you:

> ➤ enhance your reputation
> ➤ keep your customers coming back
> ➤ serve as a marketing strategy

Enhance your reputation

The customer who had a problem—and then had that problem fixed, by you or your crew—is the best friend any business owner can have. People love to discuss the challenges they have when they're out shopping; nothing travels faster than bad news. But if your store is the place that fixes problems, that handles situations, and that leaves customers happy, you'll shine by comparison.

Keep your customers coming back

People have short tempers. I'm particularly guilty of this; if I feel like a store is treating me badly, you'd better believe I won't go back there. There are plenty of other stores out there, some of which would value my business and treat me the way I think I should be treated. I don't have to put up with lousy treatment, and neither does any other customer out there.

Fixing customers' problems is one way to make them feel special and give them the treatment they feel they deserve. If you don't fix it, you don't get another chance. It's too easy to go somewhere else, and I don't care where you are or what you sell. The global marketplace is one computer keyboard away, and no matter what you offer, they can get it cheaper on eBay. The reason people still visit brick-and-mortar retailers is that they value the experience and the relationship. It's up to you to make it a good one. Damage control is essential to that.

Serve as a marketing strategy

This might not be immediately obvious, but having a strong and effective damage control policy can help you attract business down the road. My favorite story about this comes out of the travel industry.

A few years ago, (okay, more than a few; it's my book. I get to pretend that I'm younger than I am!) there was an airline called Eastern Airlines. Eastern Airlines was one of the major carriers in this country, but ran into some financial trouble along the way. They abruptly stopped services one day: flights cancelled, passengers stranded, the whole bit. It was an unmitigated disaster.

But one smart travel agent had her ear to the ground, and she knew what was coming. Just before the news hit, she had a pizza party and kept her agents working around the clock. They spent crazy hours on the phone, rebooking all of their clients onto other flights—*before* Eastern made the announcement that it was shutting down.

When the news hit, of course all of her clients called the agency in an absolute panic. What was going to happen to their vacation plans? How could they make their business trips? She was able to smile and tell them they'd all already been taken care of, and here were their alternate arrangements. It was a brilliant bit of customer service.

The good news didn't stop there. Of course, all of those customers could tell their friends and colleagues how well "they" had handled the Eastern Airline crisis. That type of word of mouth is so valuable. That became evident when this agent was out soliciting other business in the future. She could ask, with full confidence, "How did your current agent handle the Eastern Airline meltdown?" and point to her own agency's performance in comparison. Her damage control served as a valuable marketing point.

The other side of damage control

Having a damage control policy minimizes jerks. I wish it eliminated the jerks completely, but it doesn't. As far as I can tell, there's no legal way to completely eliminate jerks.

However, there are those customers who aren't going to be happy no matter what you or your employees do. They come in with a chip on their shoulder and they're determined to make somebody miserable. Guess who's in their crosshairs? You (or one of your crew members).

Here's one tidbit to remember: when you get that just-can't-be-pleased-customer who's having a fit and carrying on and screaming about how he's going to tell all of his friends how horrible your business is, you can relax. That person doesn't have any friends. If God himself came down to fix the problem, this person still wouldn't be happy. You can't fix everything. Let it go, get the person out of your place, and move on with the day.

When dealing with irate customers, one thing I will not tolerate is abuse to my employees. If a customer crosses that line and starts verbally or physically abusing my crew, I throw them out of the store. If I'm not there when it happens, I call them and tell them they're not welcome back. My employees are the most important thing to me. They built my business, just like your employees built yours. No way am I going to let some random wing nut with issues come in and treat them like garbage.

This is a huge issue for your employees. You can't do anything better for your employees' morale than to protect them from these types of individuals. One out-of-control customer can completely destroy your team's spirit unless you step in and prevent it from happening. That's the other kind of damage control policy, and I think it's just as important as the first one.

Dave's Dozen

1. Everyone makes mistakes. It happens in every business. You need to be prepared.

2. Having a clear policy that everyone—employees and customers alike—knows and understands is essential and eliminates problems.

3. Understand that customers never care whose fault the problem is. They just want the problem fixed.

4. Give your employees the power to resolve problems on the spot. Provide the freedom and support to make employees confident in their problem solving skills.

5. Let customers tell you how to fix the problem.

6. Learn this sentence: "I'm sorry there was a screwup; what would you like me to do to fix it?

7. Get in the habit of calling your customers to resolve problems.

8. Remember that, as an added bonus, calling customers can provide great insight into what's going on in your stores.

9. Always act on what customers tell you is going wrong; ignore them, and you've accomplished nothing except irritating your customers.

10. A damage control policy can help you keep customers, make more money, and avoid big headaches.

11. Having a good damage control policy can set you apart from the competition; it can also serve as a marketing strategy.

12. Understand and accept that some customers cannot be pleased no matter what you do.

13. Make sure to protect your employees from jerks. That's the other side of damage control!

Chapter 7:

Treat Your Best Customers Better

Identifying your best customers

There's some argument out there about the exact percentage, but everyone agrees that most of a retailer's business is supported by a small, loyal core of customers. Some will say 80 percent of your sales comes from 20 percent of your customers, while others say it's 75/25—a few even claim it's more like 90/10. The numbers aren't the important part; the concept is. What you need to do is identify that small, loyal group of customers and focus on making them happy.

Since you've been collecting customer data, this should be easy. Most POS systems can easily generate reports detailing who is in the store the most often, who spends the most, and what they buy. That's a great starting point. In this section, we're going to look at what you can do with that information.

Staying in touch

If you want to keep your most-valued customers coming back, you've got to let them know how much you value them. And to do that, you have to stay in touch with them. All of the things you do to maintain a relationship in your personal life, you need to do with your customers! That includes the call after the date, the holiday card to the friend halfway across the country, and the e-mail you send "just because."

The secret is to constantly stay in relevant communication with your customers. You need both elements: the frequency and the relevancy. If you seldom, if ever, reach out to your customers, you can't build a relationship with them. If it's not relevant, you're going to annoy the heck out of them.

There are three primary ways we stay in touch with our customers:

> We call them.
> We send them mailings.
> We e-mail them.

Each of these strategies works on the same premise: that we only contact our customers when we have information they'd be interested in. Keeping it relevant is crucial. Send them the stuff they want, the things they want to learn about, or the things they will benefit from. Don't send garbage!

The more you communicate with your customers, the more your customers will communicate with you. This is a good thing and a bad thing; you'll get more business, but you're also going to hear about each and every thing that goes wrong in your company. You've got to be able to respond to these communications, especially when it comes to e-mail, which customers fully expect to be answered in a nanosecond!

It takes effort, but it's totally worth it; the customers you take care of, especially after they've had a problem, become your best asset. They tell everyone what a great place you are and how you took care of them. You can't buy that kind of advertising.

Saying thank you

Here's one of the most vital tips I can offer you. If you want the secret to treating your most highly valued customers better, it boils down to two words: **Thank you.** If you want to treat your better customers better, say thank you to them. There's the everyday sort of thank you that happens during the course of business—cashiers should thank the customer for coming in, for example—but you want to go above and beyond that.

The best way to say thank you is to make it tangible. Make it real. Words may be powerful, but they fade quickly. You can't put words up on a shelf and look at them later and smile. You can't show off words. Words simply don't have the same impact as tangible objects and concrete action.

Here are some ways to make your thanks real:

The power of pie

Every year at Thanksgiving, we give our best customers an apple pie. It's a sweet little way to say thank you, and who doesn't like pie? A lot of people think this is really goofy, and we get laughed at a bit, but by and large people like pie. As an added bonus, this thank you is so unusual that the AP picked up on it, and Dave's Soda and Pet City was featured in the national press a few years ago. Not a bad return for a simple pie.

Holiday coupons

There is absolutely, positively no better way to say thank you than to give someone free money. That's what we do every year, during the holiday season. We use our database to identify our best customers. The biggest spenders get a ten dollar coupon, and the not-quite-as-big-but-still substantial customers get a five dollar coupon that they can use for anything. There are no strings attached—no minimum purchase, no time requirement.

Every now and then a cashier will call the office to let us know that someone's about to make a four dollar and ninety-nine cent purchase with that five dollar coupon, and we assure them that that's okay. That's more than okay; it's kind of the point. We love our customers so much that we're willing to give them free money. It blows the crew away, but there's no better way to drive the value of our culture home than to demonstrate it in action.

You might say we're nuts, but we get about a 60 percent return rate on these coupons. Our customers are delighted with them. It's just good business. I can almost guarantee that the customers who receive these coupons do a certain portion of their holiday shopping in our stores.

A side note on this thank you: every now and then, I'll get a phone call. It'll go something like this: "My friend got a five-dollar coupon, and I didn't—but I'm in there all the time!" After a little investigation, it generally turns out that the friend spent a gazillion dollars in our store, while the caller didn't, or if they've been in as much as they say they have, they've failed to use their Club Dave Card. We explain that, and often those callers become die-hard Club Dave Card users.

Clean up

Springtime might be beautiful in Paris, but it's pretty darn nasty in Massachusetts. When the February slush and the March mud arrive, our best customers receive a postcard they can bring into the store and exchange for a coupon for a free car wash. There are no strings attached. We just want our best customers to be able to have a shiny, clean car. We buy the coupons wholesale, for two dollars and twenty-five cents apiece—yet our customers receive a full value car wash worth nearly ten dollars. It's a great deal, a true reward. It also has the advantage of being totally unexpected.

Offer special services

Another great strategy for thanking your customers is to offer them special services. Not only can these services be a great way to say thank you, they often serve to draw in new customers or to demonstrate your expertise in your field. And just in case you think I'm writing this whole book to tell you how wonderful I am, here are some examples of retailers who use great thank you strategies. (I stole most of my ideas from them!)

Access to events

Opening early to allow your very best customers to come in and shop a sale before the general public gets access is a great way to say thank you. Some people love the crazy, nuthouse environment of a big sales event, so they won't take you up on it, but others will go nuts for the exclusive, special invitation feel.

Seminars

People love information. Seminars and classes of interest to your best customers are a powerful draw. Home Depot does this with their classes; they offer everything from kids' build–a-birdhouse workshops to faux-finishing demonstrations. Every business can offer some kind of seminar or class to their customers.

Saying thank you works well no matter what industry you're in. It's not always called saying thank you; there's something about corporate America that prevents us calling something by a name that accurately represents what it is. I think you might have to pay a fine or something. Anyway, another way that companies say thanks is via what's called Soft Reward programs. You see this when the airlines offer frequent-flier miles, and Hertz rental cars have the cars warmed up and waiting for you after your flight. Hotels will occasionally provide a free room, especially for those high rollers who have just dropped a bundle in the casino, or let children stay for free.

Moving more toward the retail environment, you see soft rewards appear in many ways: BJ's and other warehouse stores will open early for their best customers, while other stores offer invitation-only sales and special events. Add-on services, such as repairs, engraving, or cleanings, can serve as a soft reward for the very best customers. Even if you normally charge for these services, waiving the fee for preferred shoppers can serve as a very powerful reward.

Every business needs a distinctive way to say thank you. This can be a tangible object or concrete action, as I outlined earlier, or it can be a soft reward. The choice is yours, and you should make it based on what you know about your customers. But make no mistake: No matter what business you're in, no matter what type of organization you have, you can do this! More importantly, you have to do this. We're in head-to-head competition with larger companies each and every day. The only way to win the war is to make our customers love us. Saying thank you, often and regularly, is one way to make this happen.

A closer look at loyalty cards

There's not a customer anywhere on this planet who doesn't love a good deal. Frequent-shopper clubs, discount programs, and loyalty cards are great programs to generate repeat business, not to mention say thank you to your customers. However, you have to remember one thing. These programs are a tool. They do not, in and of themselves, create loyalty. The only thing that will create loyalty is your relationship with your customers. We are loyal to people, not stores.

Of course, customers love frequent-shopper programs. If you're going to have a frequent-shopper program, take the time to think it through. How will this work, and what can you do with your frequent-shopper program to treat your best customers better?

Let's look at an example. Every dog food company has a frequent-buyer program. They're pretty simple, by and large: Buy ten twenty-pound bags, and your next bag is free. No problem, right? You normally buy twenty-pound bags of dog food, so you sign up for the card. Every eleventh bag is free. You're happy, your dog is happy, and your retailer is happy; life is grand.

Except one day, six bags into your total, you're short on cash. Maybe you forgot your wallet at home. Maybe you spent more than you meant to at lunch that day. Either way, you're at the store, you need to get dog food, and you only have enough money on hand to buy a ten-pound bag of dog food. What happens? Generally, with most frequent buyer programs, you're out of luck. You can always buy nine more ten-pound bags, of course, and get your eleventh ten-pound bag free, but the purchase does nothing toward your normal routine of twenty-pound bags.

How convenient is that for the customer? They now have to keep track of two sets of purchases. If you run a special on forty-pound economy-size bags, will your shoppers shy away from the deal, for fear of screwing up their frequent-buyer card? Some will because it's just not convenient for the customer. Few, if any, will keep track of multiple frequent-buyer cards. Life is complicated enough!

A truly customer-focused company wouldn't even consider making life that complicated for the customer. It's too much hassle. Instead, it's important to find a way to make life easier for the customer. That's what we did with the frequent-buyer program at Dave's Soda and Pet City. Instead of the situation outlined above, we want you to buy a certain number of pounds of dog food. As long as you buy two hundred pounds of dog food, we don't care if you buy it ten pounds at a time or forty pounds at a time; we just guarantee to give you a free twenty pounds when you buy two hundred pounds. It can be wet food, it can be dry food, it can be biscuits or treats. The category doesn't matter.

This is easy for the customer. We keep track of everything with our database. They don't have to fuss around with multiple cards or coupons. It's virtually effortless. We also make it fun. We put "Is this your freebie?" stickers on their bag. It makes customers smile when they get their free bag; I can't tell you how many times it's been an unexpected surprise for our customers. They love it.

I truly believe we spend way more on our existing customers than recruiting new ones, and the loyalty program is one of the ways we do this. Never forget: your customers can always go anywhere. You want them to come back to you. Loyalty and frequent-buyer programs can be a great competitive tool in that struggle.

It's worked really well for us. It took a little longer to get some knuckle-headed vendors to come on board, but once they did, they saw that it works. Not only does it work, but customers tend to buy more, and they buy more higher-margin items, which is good news for everyone.

So the lesson to take away here is this: Frequent buyers programs are great, but they don't create loyalty in and of themselves. If you're going to have this kind of program, think about how you can make it of the most value to the customer.

Effective frequent-buyer programs have to:

> be easy to use and understand,
> offer attainable goals,
> encourage repeat business.

Dave's Dozen

1. It is incredibly important to use your database to reach out to your best customers.
2. To treat your best customers better, you need to know who they are and what they buy or use.
3. The earliest days of a new customer relationship are the most critical.
4. Say thank you.
5. Make your thank yous unique and memorable.
6. Tangible gifts and concrete actions are powerful ways to say thanks.
7. Soft rewards, like opening early and offering special events, can be done by any retailer.
8. Think through your loyalty cards: are you making it easy for the customer?
9. Add an element of fun to your loyalty card/frequent-buyer programs.

10. Targeted campaigns, such as phone, e-mail, and direct mail, are fabulous ways to build relationships with your customers.

11. Keep communications relevant and of interest to your customer.

12. The more you communicate with your customers, the more they'll expect an immediate response when they contact you, so be prepared for that.

13. The customer who has a problem that you fix becomes your best advocate.

Ok, now I want you to do me a favor. Put down the book and get online. Visit me at

www.DaveRatner.com

I want to talk to you about the stuff you're reading about. And I promise, cross my heart, I'm not trying to sell you anything!

Part Two:

Have Employees Who Know How to
Implement Your Customer Service Policies

Chapter 8:

Hire Really Nice People Who "Get It"

When I first started writing this book, I thought I knew what the title to this section was going to be. It was going to be "Every employee must know that their number one priority is to make sure the customer comes back!"

That's a duh, right? Of course you want the customer to come back. Then I saw Robert Cooper speak, and he pointed out that not only do you want the customer to come back, you want them to recommend your business to their friends. That's brilliant, and it only took me thirty-two years to catch on. Look how much time I've saved you!

Of course we want customers who come back. We can't run a store without repeat business. But that's not enough anymore. Instead, we need customers who tell their family and friends about us and who encourage them to come on into our place and check it out. A huge part of this comes down to the people you've got working for you.

Think about it; you can have the best merchandise, the shiniest, nicest-looking store, and great prices, but if your customers don't like your crew, you're going to be out of business so fast your head won't even have a chance to spin.

It is impossible to say how important your crew is. The people behind the register, stocking the shelves, saying hello, and carrying orders out to the car are more than frontline employees. They are the walking, talking, living, breathing embodiment of your brand. In this section, we're going to look at how to find the right people, how to keep and motivate them, and how, when you get a bad apple, to let them go with a minimum of grief and heartache.

Hire for attitude

Creating a great crew starts from day one, when you hire people for your business. Sure, you can hire any old person and attempt to transform him or her into your ideal employee, but why not make life easy for yourself? Make a conscious decision to hire the very nicest people you can. This sounds like another one of my no-brainers, but too many times as business owners, we are so busy that we almost go on autopilot. We make decisions—critical decisions—without taking the time to give them the thought and consideration they deserve.

Hiring is one of those decisions. Be slow to hire, quick to fire. I might sound a little cocky here, but if I know one thing after thirty-two years, it's this: every single time I've made a bad hire, it's because I hired quickly. I can't even imagine how many people I've hired over the years: hundreds, if not thousands. And I've learned that when you hire quickly, you make mistakes. Take your time.

What are you doing when you're taking all this time to hire? One of the things you should be doing is considering the attitude of the people you're bringing on board your crew. We almost take this to extremes at our stores. You can be as inept as you can be, a real bumbling idiot, but if you've got a nice smile and a good personality, we'll hire you. If you're friendly and outgoing and gregarious, we'll give you a shot. We hire for attitude, not for skills. But this isn't a free pass, you understand. I can't tell you the number of super-nice, genuine sweethearts I've had to fire, because they just could not, no matter what, get the hang of running the register.

But skills, by and large, can be taught. There's not much that happens in a retail environment that someone can't be trained to do. I'd say this is true for the vast majority of people reading this book;

unless you've got an extremely technical position to fill, you're better off hiring for attitude than for skills.

When you are hiring for that technical position, of course, you need to put a higher premium on skills. I want the people in my accountant department to be right more than I want them to be friendly. But in an ideal world, they would be friendly and right. The positive effect someone with an upbeat, outgoing attitude can have on the rest of your company is amazing.

Beyond the impact attitude has on your organization, you have to consider the way employees' attitudes affect the public. Anyone who has contact with customers absolutely, positively has to have a friendly, outgoing attitude. (A sidenote here: Never, ever, ever, ever let the credit department talk to your customers. If there was any justice in this world, the credit department would be known as the Sales Prevention Department. It's unbelievable how many great relationships have been ruined by credit departments, and I don't care what industry you're in, what business you're in; you know it's true! If you have a problem with one of your accounts, let the account manager deal with it directly. They have an existing relationship with the customer and can most likely capitalize on that relationship to get things back in order. That's much better than a credit department employee making a cold call with bad news!)

If one of your employees has both a bad attitude and contact with the public, you've got to get rid of this person. This is the "quick to fire" part of the equation. When you have employees who don't want to be in your business, who are negative, who complain constantly, and who just never have a good day, let them go. Fire them. You don't need them.

In fact, you can't tolerate these kinds of employees. They're a type of cancer. They draw everyone else down. The negativity that they exude infects everyone else, and before you know it, your great crew is full of surly, snarling psychos. No one wants to shop in a store like that, nor trust their business to an office full of grouches. We draw a clear line: If you're not happy here, we don't want you.

All things being equal, we like nice people. Life's too short to deal with the surly, the cranky, the incompetent, and the just plain nasty. Yet those are exactly the people many business owners hire to work the front lines!

Employees are the most critical component of any store. Dave's wouldn't be Dave's without my people. They're the reason we're successful: every smile, every greeting, every bag of dog food carried out of the store; it all adds up to make a place customers love so much that they'd feel guilty about going anywhere else.

What makes a good employee?

I'm asked this question more than you could ever imagine: sometimes by job seekers, other times by retailers who want to re-create what we do in their own stores.

You see, it's not the fixtures that make Dave's. It's certainly not our merchandising efforts. We carry great products, and we have good prices, but we're not the cheapest store in town. We draw in the customers for one simple reason: we treat our customers better than they'll be treated anywhere else. It's our employees that make that possible. Good employees.

> - like what they're doing;
> - like the company they're working for;
> - understand that their main job is to make the customer come back.

This, of course, is in addition to the basic stuff you expect from any human being: they're honest, they're cheerful, and they don't spontaneously break into show tunes or country music.

That's a good employee. You can have a good store with good employees. To take it to the next level, you want great employees. Great employees have all the qualities of a good employee, plus one essential quality:

Great employees are champions of your store. They go above and beyond in order to make your store better. I'm blessed to have lots of great employees. If I started giving examples of how great my employees are, you'd have five hundred pages of text to plow through, and I'd still wind up leaving someone out!

You see, great employees act independently to make your store better. My people are great at going that extra mile. They go to the customer's house to help set up the fish tank. They'll call the vet to see if this guinea pig medicine will react with that guinea pig medicine. They'll talk to customers for hours about the best treats and toys for their cats. And they do all of this without making a big deal of it. If you ask any of my crew about it, they'll just shrug, smile, and say, "That's what we're here for!"

A great employee will think about your business. I've got one employee, Matt, who excels at this. If fish sales go into a slump, Matt's going to find out why. He'll investigate what's going on and what can be done to remedy the situation. I don't tell him to do this. He just does it.

A great employee loves your company. They love what they're doing. They continually strive to make things better. You have to have good employees. It is my fervent hope that you all find great employees as well.

It's okay to have fun

I almost gave this Dave-ism its own category, but it's really part of doing business with people who are nice. We all like to have fun, but you can't really have fun without nice people. Well, you can, but that's another book entirely.

Coming back to retail, your store has to be more fun than the next guy's. If there's one thing we've done really well, it's creating a fun environment in our stores, and I'll tell you, hands down, that's one of the most powerful things you can do to drive business.

Listen, there's not one retailer reading this book who has a product that the shopper can't get someplace else, and usually cheaper. That's the nature of the market today. Mega retailers and deep discount chains operate at such a volume that they can undercut us on price every time. The Internet means customers don't even have to leave their houses in order to get what they want. If we want to succeed as retailers, we've got to do something that sets us apart from both the chains and the Web. We have to do something different. We need to do it better.

There are two things we can do. We can offer superior customer service, which I go on and on about in another part of this book, and we can have fun. Let's talk about the fun, specifically about what your crew can do to create a fun atmosphere.

Fun people

Your crew makes all the difference in the world when it comes to creating a fun environment. This starts right from day one, so you want to hire friendly people who will enjoy working for you. Someone who comes to work smiling is far more likely to create a fun environment than a perpetually gloomy guy.

Let your people have fun. It's okay if they get excited about an event. Enthusiasm is contagious; if your crew is enjoying themselves and having a good time, your customers will, too. Think about how many times you've had a retail experience negatively affected by one person in the store, like the sales associate who'd rather be anywhere else or the cashier who couldn't look you in the eye.

Get rid of those people. Hire fun people. Give them the tools they need to create a fun atmosphere. This can be really simple: If you've got a cashier who can't resist giving little kids in the checkout stickers, make sure she's got stickers to give. If your best merchandiser wants to have a beach-themed event, rustle up some palm trees. Why do you think the bank tellers at the drive up window have dog biscuits?

Don't hire out of desperation

Part of being slow to hire, quick to fire is never, ever hiring someone out of desperation. I know, I know. I can hear you from here: sometimes it happens. You've got two guys running a store, and one guy quits with no notice. What are you going to do? You need a warm body, preferably one capable of moving independently and with a face that doesn't scare small children. So you hire somebody, anybody, to fill that position and fast.

I know what it's like, because I've done it, too. I don't think there's a retailer anywhere on the planet who has never done this, which is too bad. It's too bad, because it's almost always a mistake.

I've got a great crew now. I like to brag about my guys. They do a fantastic job, and I have to say I'm very blessed with the quality of people I have working for me. But we've gone through a lot of pits to get the cherries. There are all types of people out there—thieves, liars, and screwballs—and some days it seems like they're all determined to work at my store. I've hired my fair share and then some. But I'll tell you one thing: every single time I've hired someone out of desperation, it's been a mistake. Sure, I'll find some winners on my own, but if I make a fast decision to fill a spot because I need somebody there, it is almost invariably a problem down the road. I'd say ninety-nine times out of a hundred, making a decision out of desperation causes you more headaches than it solves.

Let me give you an example of a time when I hired someone out of desperation. I have four stores, and one body. No matter how much energy I've got, I just cannot be everywhere, all the time, and that's why I've got managers. By and large, I have great managers, but at the time this story occurred, that wasn't the case. At least not at one of our stores.

This store was just not performing. It was imperative that I take care of it quickly. I needed a manager who could come in and turn things around. I needed someone who could shake things up.

I was counting on a manager to raise the level of customer service in that particular store to the Dave standard. This was not a long-term goal. This had to happen fast. It needed to happen now, if it couldn't happen yesterday.

We jumped right into it, doing a whole bunch of interviews. One of the interviewees was a woman who'd been a customer service manager at the local TJ Maxx. My wife is a TJ Maxx shopper; she'd encountered this woman before and had a good customer service experience with her. That was encouraging—you don't stay married as long as I have without learning to listen to your wife!—and during the interview, I heard more that I liked. The candidate told us about her focus on customer service, and how she knew customer service was paramount at Dave's, and how she wanted to be part of that culture. It was exactly what I needed to hear. The fact that I really, really, really needed someone didn't hurt, either. I hired her.

Everything was going fine. I was starting to see some of the hoped-for turnaround in that store. Then it happened.

A customer, who had been in the store earlier that day with her sick guinea pig, came to the door. The same employee who tried to help her earlier in the day was still there. The customer needed medicine for her guinea pig, and she needed it now. We carried the medicine in the store. The customer had the cash on her to pay for the medicine. But there was a problem.

You see, it was exactly 8:02, and the store closed at 8:00.

My new manager, who'd given such great customer service to my wife, wouldn't let the customer into the store. The woman who'd gone on and on about the value of customer service and how important it was to her would not open the door for this customer. Instead, she told the customer—and, presumably, her sick guinea pig—that the store was closed, and sent her on her way.

The next morning, of course, the woman called me. She was furious. The store had only been closed for two minutes, but my employees had refused to help her. When she went to the local veterinarian's office, she told me, they were also closing up for the day, but they were willing to go the extra mile and get her the medicine her guinea pig needed.

I apologized, up and down, and thanked the customer for letting me know about this situation. Then I got off the phone and went looking for this manager. When I found her, I had one question: What in the world had she been thinking? The answer was from a big business, corporate mind-set, where the focus is on the bottom line, and the customer is forgotten. Here's what she told me: "We were closed," she said. "Asset security had to be considered. After all, the registers were open. The cash was right there. Who knows what could have happened? Besides which," she added, in case I'd forgotten the fact, "we were closed."

Setting aside the fact that I didn't think it was likely that this customer was going to turn into a mad ninja-criminal, intent on emptying every register while holding onto a sniffling rodent, I had to ask her why she didn't consider other possibilities. Couldn't she have brought the medicine out to the customer? Couldn't she have delivered the medicine to the customer's home? Couldn't she have simply given the customer the medicine? Wasn't there some way she could have made that customer happy so she didn't leave our store with a sick animal and no way to take care of it?

She just didn't get it. We were closed.

I had to fire her. It was the worst possible time for me to have to do this; the store still needed a manager, and as I'd just learned, that wasn't a position you can fill in a hurry. But if I kept her on after that, when I knew she fundamentally, at a core level, didn't understand what customer service was all about, I'd have been making a huge mistake. If I didn't fire her, every single thing I'd been preaching about customer service to my employees would go right out the window. You have to reinforce your words with your actions, even when it hurts.

That's why you shouldn't hire out of desperation. Chances are you'll still do it. Heck, chances are *I'll* still do it. But you've absolutely, positively got to keep it to a minimum. Fine yourself two thousand dollars every time you hire someone out of desperation. Write the check to your favorite charity, or give it to your kid and send them off to the mall. That two grand is gone, but it may be nothing compared to what hiring someone out of desperation will cost you in the long run.

Always be on the lookout for good employees

Turnover is part of business, especially the retail business. As much as we like to find and keep good employees, the reality is that there will always be a need for new people. Some employees move on to other jobs. Others leave the workforce, to retire or raise children or study transcendental meditation. Then you've got those who steal from you, or are rude to the customers, or are just so incompetent that you have to let them go.

No matter what the reason, the fact remains that there will come a time when you have to replace someone. There's an art and a science to recruiting, and I'll get to that in just a minute, but first I want to talk about a basic premise that can make your business better. If you don't adopt any other strategy I've mentioned in this book, use this one.

Keep your eyes open for good employees. I realize you're in your store a lot, but when you're not, you need to be on the lookout. When my wife and I are out shopping, and we get great customer service, we make a point of telling the sales associate, "Hey, if you're not happy here, come work for us. We'd love to have you."

My stores rise and fall based on the quality of the people I have working in them. We want the best of the best to be working for us, so we actively recruit. People need to be happy in their jobs. If I see someone with the attitude and skills we need, why not give them the opportunity to be happy with us?

By the same token, some of the best potential employees might already be in your store. We've found that lots of our best employees are our customers. When we place an ad looking for help, we invariably get two or three resumes that say, "I've been shopping at Dave's for years, and I like how you do business; I want to be part of that."

As an aside: That's why it is crucial to respond to all resumes; you never know if it's a customer who's applying to you. You don't want to tick them off and lose their business by ignoring their resume. That doesn't mean you have to hire them, of course, but you do absolutely have to acknowledge them.

Recruiting Employees

If you have a reputation for being the best at what you do, quality people will be drawn to you. That's the first, and probably most critical, aspect of attracting top-notch employees. That being said, there's an art to classifieds, or at least there is the way we do them. Here are a few examples of recent ads we've run:

Manager Dave's is moving to a much larger location. We need an experienced retail manager who will make sure our store continues to be voted "Best of Springfield." If you are a manager who hates answering to a hundred bosses, hates working sixty hours, and hates not being able to make your own decisions, then this could be the perfect life for you. Send resumes to Dave@DaveRatner.com.

Bookkeeper/Comptroller Dave's needs an experienced bookkeeper /office manager for very busy, six-person office. Duties include general ledger through trial balance, auditing the four stores, payroll, insurance, etc. Knowledge of purchase orders, inventory, and cash management as well as the ability to manage a zillion projects at once. We have had three bookkeepers in thirty-one years. We want a long-term relationship! E-mail Dave@DaveRatner.com.

Cashier/Customer Service Dave's needs full- and part-time folks who give great customer service. We are "Best of the Valley" because of the people who work at Dave's; excellent pay and benefits even for part-timers!! E-mail Dave@DaveRatner.com.

Managers, Key Holders, Shift Supervisors Voted "Best Pet Shop" for the fifth time! Dave's is growing! We need folks who give great customer service to keep the streak going. We offer BIG company benefits in a small company setting. Full-time and part-time positions available. E-mail Dave@DaveRatner.com.

As you can see, these aren't the usual classified ads. You've got a limited amount of space to demonstrate your personality and share the information you have to get out to job seekers. So we always brag about our store. We're proud of the business we've built, and we want the people who work for us to be proud of it as well. If you can't be enthused about working with us, we're probably not the employer for you. Notice that we talk about the "Best of" awards; quality people want to be associated with quality outfits. Your reputation is the best tool for recruiting employees. If you've been honored or voted the best of something, let people know. It makes a real impression and might inspire the best of the best to seek you out over your competitor.

You've got to be creative when recruiting employees. Now most newspapers who offer classified advertising automatically list your ads online. If not, explore what online sites are popular with the people who are most likely to make good employees.

It doesn't hurt to be a little sneaky. I run recruiting advertisements on the radio. It's a guerilla strategy, and it's incredibly effective. You need to be where your desired employees are. If you need young employees, advertise on the alternative or indie stations. Be smart about this. Create the ad using the language that appeals to your would-be hires: use their slang and a wry sense of humor. You'll be a more appealing employer.

We also work with a program that helps physically-challenged people find jobs. There are two reasons I do this. First, here I am, with three healthy kids. (Two of them are for sale, by the way! I'm keeping the one who's already through college.) I've been incredibly blessed, and I don't ever want to take that for granted. Second, it's a great business decision: I get great employees, and the community thinks we're great for providing the jobs. It's really win/win/win.

Another way we find employees is by working with a program sponsored by the local jail. Non-violent offenders who have paid their debt to society often have a difficult time finding employment. We've had great success working with this program. It might be worth exploring similar programs in your region.

When you recruit, make sure to

> match the pay offered by your largest competitors;
> offer benefits (health insurance is essential);
> be honest in your description of job duties;
> don't do a bait and switch—the position available should match what you're recruiting for!

Using your crew as a recruiting tool

I'm really blessed to have crew members who have been with me for ten, twelve, or fifteen years. When I'm interviewing someone, I tell them, "Go talk to so and so; she's been with me for thirteen years, she'll tell you what it's like to be here." There's an authenticity and credibility that comes from your employees. There's no other way to get that. Let them tell the world what you're like to work for. If you can do that confidently, you're doing a good job.

Communicating with your employees

Beginning at day one, you want to communicate with employees. The more your crew knows, the better job they'll do for you. Make life easy for yourself and your crew by letting them know what you expect of them and what they can expect from you. A no-brainer, perhaps, but one that will transform your business.

I do anonymous employee surveys to get feedback from my crew about how things are going in the stores. I learn a lot from these surveys, and you'll read more about that later, but one thing I've learned is particularly relevant here. Employees love training. I'd never suspected that. I always thought that when the vendors came in to talk about a new product or line of merchandise, my guys could take it or leave it. That's absolutely not true. Instead, according to what my own crew told me, the more information they had about the merchandise, the more effectively they could sell it. Additionally, the more they knew, the more they liked working with the merchandise. An informed sales crew is one of the best resources any retailer could wish for.

Now we always ask our vendors what they can do to help our team sell their product. This is something the big guys do all the time; there's no reason they can't give your crew the pizza party, the signs, and the training needed to move their merchandise more effectively. Don't be shy about asking for these things.

Ways to keep your crew informed:

> sales meetings as needed
> vendor-sponsored training sessions
> memos in the paycheck—everyone opens his or her paycheck

Mistakes we make with employees

Hiring out of desperation is a common mistake, but it's not the only mistake we make with our employees. Oh, no; you didn't think we were getting off that easy, did you? Here are some other things that employers are guilty of.

Ignoring essential qualifications

Some jobs require the people performing them to have certain qualities. For example, if the bulk of your business is conducted over the phone, make sure the people answering the phones have great phone voices and can have an engaging conversation. I don't want to call and talk to the state vegetable! I want to talk to a person, and I want to feel like the person is happy talking to me. Sometimes you get the impression that you're talking to a head of cabbage; if you've got coleslaw answering the phone, you're going to lose business. Replace them with someone friendly, chatty, and knowledgeable.

Overlooking the cashier

Being a cashier is not exactly a high prestige position. No one brings up their kids saying, "If you work really hard, and try with all your might, someday you might be a cashier!" Yet cashiers are among the most influential people in any retail environment. They're often the last person the customer sees. The final impression your customers have of your store is formed, almost entirely, by the cashier.

Therefore, the cashier should be a superstar. You want your very best people in this influential position. This is not a place to put your slack-jawed idiots; how often do you go through a checkout line to discover that's exactly who's working the position?

Our cashiers are absolutely critical in our database marketing efforts. That's how we get people enrolled in the Dave's Club program: our cashiers have shoppers sign up in order to receive coupons and benefits. Yet when I went to a convention, where one of my competitors was speaking, he was asked how he motivated his cashiers to get shoppers enrolled in the loyalty card program, and he replied, "Oh, we don't expect them to do that. They're only cashiers."

Ouch. How would you like to be one of his cashiers? When your boss thinks you're not quite bright enough to have someone sign up for a loyalty program, it doesn't make you feel all that good about yourself, I'm guessing.

A huge percentage of what makes a customer come back is wholly under the influence of your cashiers. They play a fantastically large role in customer retention. When you ask people what they hate about stores, almost all of their answers have to do with the cashiers. They especially hate the following things:

> ➤ waiting in line
> ➤ cashiers not knowing what they're doing
> ➤ slow cashiers
> ➤ cashier distracted and not paying attention
> ➤ cashier chewing gum
> ➤ cashier talking on the phone

It's clear you need good people on your registers. You need to pay to keep them there; otherwise, your best people will migrate to other positions where they'll make more money and get more respect.

We pay our cashiers what they deserve, and that's why our business does well.

Show me the money

Another major mistake employees make is not paying quality employees the wages they deserve. As I explained earlier, if you want quality people, you have to pay quality wages. The temptation is always there to cut costs and pay as little as you can; after all, the lower your expenses, the greater your profit. However, this mentality costs you in the long run.

Look at most of your chain retailers. What do they pay their people? Not very much. I'm not going to name names here, but it's possible to work full-time at some places and still live below the poverty line. That's a disgrace. And don't even get me started on health insurance.

The Golden Rule applies to your employees, as well. You have to be willing to pay your crew a decent wage. No one's going to give you their best efforts if you're not willing to pay them for it. Think about it. How hard would you work for minimum wage?

This is not the most popular position in the world. The stockholders of Costco recently raked CEO Jim Sinegal over the coals for overpaying his employees. Costco employees earn almost 42 percent more than employees at Sam's Club, and that raises concerns for people who think the bottom line is the only place to find important information. Yet Costco has incredibly low turnover among its employees. When you look at employees who have been with the company more than a year, the turnover rate is less than 6 percent! Sinegal has this to say: "Our attitude has always been that if you hire good people and provide good wages and good jobs and, more than that—if you provide careers—that good things will happen to your company. I think we can say that that has been proved by the quality of people that we have and how they have built our organization."

It works for him, and I have to say it works for me.

Dave's Dozen

1. A good employee likes his or her job, likes the company, and understands that making the customer come back is the number one priority.
2. A great employee goes above and beyond that point.
3. Remember to hire people who are nice and to let them have fun!
4. Cashiers are critically important: choose carefully!
5. Always hire for attitude. Skills can be taught.
6. Keep your eyes open: you never know when you'll find a great employee.
7. Use a multi-pronged approach to find employees: newspaper, online, radio, community programs.
8. Don't be afraid to brag about your store in your advertising; quality employees want to work for the best!
9. Never hire out of desperation.
10. Make sure you hire people who have the essential qualifications they'll need for the job.
11. Be honest and up-front about the type of company you are.
12. Communicate your expectations clearly.
13. Be prepared to match or surpass the pay and benefits offered by your competitors.

Chapter 9:

Involve Employees in Creating Policies So They're Invested

The employee manual

Every business needs an employee manual. This is a non-negotiable item: you've got to have one, and it's got to be good. Otherwise, you're going to be working for the first person who decides to sue you. It's business suicide not to have a good employee manual.

Some places to look for sample employee manuals include:

> Chamber of Commerce
> State Business Association
> Employer's Association
> Industry Associations

You can find lots of examples online. There's absolutely no reason for a business owner not to have an employee manual. You simply have to have one.

Things to include in your Employee Manual:

> company values statement
> sexual harassment policy
> anti-discrimination policy

91

Let your crew set the standard

Certain aspects of your store culture should come from your employees. What does that mean? Everyone likes to be empowered. Everyone likes to have a say. You can really improve your business by giving some of that authority to your crew.

Get a bunch of your staff together, and let them set the standards. No one likes to be told what to do, but the rules are a lot easier to take if you have a hand in creating them. For example, in our stores, the employees set the penalties for some things. If an employee is a no-call/no-show, he or she is immediately fired. That's not my decision; this decision came from my guys. It may be harsh, but it's directly from my crew. Why are they so adamant about no-call/no-show penalties? Largely because they're the ones who get screwed when someone blows off work and doesn't call.

Another thing that the employees decided was the maximum amount a person could earn in any one position. You might have a guy who's the world's best floor mopper. He might mop floors for you and do a fantastic job at it, but that's all he does. If he stays with you, however, and gets regular raises, eventually he'll be making more money than anyone else in the store!

So we've got salary caps. If you're a floor mopper, and you want to stay a floor mopper, you can do that, but you do it knowing that the maximum amount you're ever going to make mopping floors is X dollars per hour. Every position has a cap, from the stockroom to the front office, and everywhere in between. Managers can still give bonuses if someone's doing an awesome job, but that upper cap on a position remains firm.

Employee suggestions

Your employees can also be a great source of information. They all shop. Ask them to keep an eye open. If they see a great merchandising idea or display strategy—even if it's from outside your category—it could be adapted to your store. What is the customer service like at other places they shop? What do other retailers do better than you?

You may wish to have an incentive program for employee suggestions. Some retailers swear by this. I've tried it, with mixed results. The first time I tried it, I said, "For any suggestion we use, I'll pay you ten dollars."

The result? A nightmare! About eight hundred thousand suggestions, each dumber than the last. I should have told them I'd charge them if the ideas were useless; it would have saved me a lot of headaches.

Still, you want to get all the input and creativity you can, so we keep coming back to the idea. The trick is getting it right. Earlier this year, we'd set up a new program. I started by letting sixteen key employees know what the store's gross margin percentage was. The deal was this: for every percentage point that the gross margin rose during a six-month period, I'd give them a bonus worth 5 percent of the salary they'd earned during that time. It was a total flop. It absolutely did not go anywhere.

I still wound up handing out checks to reward the efforts that were made, as if we'd achieved a 1 percent increase. It cost me a ton of money but I thought it was worth it because I'd have sixteen happy employees, right? Wrong. That's when the experience really began to leave a sour taste in my mouth. After handing out those checks, exactly one employee wrote me a thank-you note. One out of sixteen. Mr. and Ms. Reader, if someone pays you a bonus, if someone does something nice for you, if someone goes the extra mile, write a thank-you note. The people handing out the money are people, too, and a little appreciation will go a long way.

We're going to rework the incentive program again. This time we'll include all the full-time employees, and we're going to structure it so it applies to one individual store, rather than the organization as a whole. I think there's real value in the idea: it's just the execution we haven't quite nailed down yet.

So that's formal incentives. We have an informal incentive program, too. All of my managers are empowered, when an employee goes above and beyond and really does a fantastic job, to open the cash register and reward them on the spot. There's nothing like some immediate cold, hard cash to reinforce that "these are the behaviors we want to see." It's the type of program you can implement immediately, and you'll see almost instantaneous results.

The employee survey

Here's something that only took me twenty-eight years to figure out. (Hey, what can I say? I'm a fast learner!) Do anonymous employee surveys. Find out what you do that ticks them off. Find out what they like about you. This can be very raw, in-your-face kind of stuff, and I've got to tell you, it's not a whole lot of fun. But this is something you have to do if you're going to grow as an owner, as a manager, and as an employer.

Why is this important? Honestly, it comes down to a simple formula: Happy employees create happy customers. You know why you want happy customers; they keep your business going strong. Having happy employees helps make it easier to have those happy customers.

You can make up your own survey, or you can Google employee surveys and pick from what you find there. Most employer associations offer an anonymous survey form. You should do this; everybody needs a report card. Some of what I read made me feel good, of course. Some, not so much. I learned a bunch of stuff I never expected, including:

> I have employees who are scared to death of me.
> I had a bad habit of coming down on employees in front of other employees.
> I was not always cheerful. Being cheerful when you don't feel like it can be very challenging, but you have to do it. Employees are incredibly sensitive to the owner's mood.
> I would, many times, forget to let the manager do the manager's job.

That last one was a real problem for me, I'll admit it. This is probably my weakest point. But once you've asked your employees to identify problems, you've got to be willing to address them. Otherwise, the exercise is worthless, and you've heard all this stuff you really didn't want to hear for no reason whatsoever, and the next time you do a survey, you won't get good feedback.

I have a cousin who works for a Fortune 100 company, and she tells me that they do employee surveys all the time. However, this company never acts on any of the information they learn from the survey. The result? None of the employees take the survey seriously because they know upper management isn't going to change anything, no matter what they say on the survey. It's just a big joke.

If you don't want your survey to be a big, time-wasting joke, you need to act on the information provided to you. My employees told me I had a bad habit of walking into the store and instantly barking orders. I wouldn't go through the manager; I'd just leap in and take over myself. So here's what I did to remedy that situation: I made a deal with my crew. If they find me attempting to direct things without going through the manager, I've got to pay them five dollars on the spot. Of course, this doesn't go for safety issues or emergencies—if you're about to fall off a ladder, I'm going to yell "Look out!"—but other than that, you'd better believe my crew holds me to it.

Dave's Dozen

1. Have a fantastic employee manual and require your crew to read it.
2. Make sure your employee manual includes your company values statement, as well as your anti-sexual harassment and anti-discrimination policies.
3. Let the crew help determine the standards of service in your store. Now you see why it's so important to have a crew that "gets it." Otherwise, this step will land you in big trouble!
4. Let your crew have a say in setting the standards for performance.

5. Work with your crew to determine salary caps for certain positions. That way the floor mopper doesn't wind up earning more money than your managers!

6. Conduct anonymous employee surveys to identify places you can improve.

7. Act on what you learn from employee surveys.

8. Be open to other employee suggestions about you, your company, your merchandise, and the vendors.

9. Offering incentives may increase the quantity of employee suggestions you receive, but doesn't necessarily improve the quality.

10. Always say thank you when someone gives you a bonus!

11. Allow your managers to give bonuses for exceptional performance.

12. On the spot incentives for great behavior often help ensure that behavior is repeated. Cash is a great incentive: everyone loves money!

13. When everyone has a say in determining policy, everyone becomes more invested in seeing that policy carried out.

Chapter 10:

Set a Good Example for Employees to Follow

If you want a great crew, you need to be a great boss. I know, I know, you're already an amazing person. That's not necessarily the same thing as being a great boss. Managing people is a skill, just like anything else, and it's an area where we can always grow and improve.

Here's some of the stuff you need to get started in the right direction.

Setting an example

In addition to the employee manual, you've got to remember something. You, Mr. or Ms. Reader, are the walking, talking, breathing employee manual. You set the standard. You're the example that your crew looks to.

A huge mistake businesses make is when the boss breaks the rules. Taking merchandise out of the store without paying for it, or "forgetting" to notify the vendor when they've packed too much merchandise into the most recent order might seem minor, but your crew notices. Employees aren't stupid: they notice when you say one thing and do another.

Anytime you take merchandise out of the store, make sure you pay for it and that your crew knows it. When I buy something, I announce it—"Tell security I paid for this!" Sure, there's a note of humor there, but I'm making a point. You have to be the ultimate example of the behavior you want to see from your crew. As an added bonus, if you make a point of letting vendors know every time they send you too much stuff, they'll believe you when you call and say you've been shorted.

Be clear with your expectations

If you want a place full of nice, friendly, fun people, you need to be really up-front and clear with your crew about what you expect from them. Tell them where you stand. Your employees aren't mind readers; they're not going to magically know what you want. You've got to tell them.

There are a lot of people I look up to in the business world. One of them is Bob Evans. Bob is a giant of a man, easily six feet six inches tall. But that's not why I look up to him (although I can't help it!) Instead, it's the way Bob communicates with his employees that really, really resonates with me. Bob's been in business a long time, and some of his staff members have been with him nearly that whole time. He has people on his team who have been working for him for eighteen years.

This is remarkable enough, but what makes it more amazing is the business Bob's in. He runs an IHOP. Turnover in the food service industry is rampant. I mean, the average length of a career in some restaurants is roughly lunch! When you see something like Bob's record, you want to know how it works, so I asked him. This is what he told me: "I am consistent. I have very high standards, but the standards remain the same every day and for every employee."

When I talked with Bob's crew members, they agreed. Bob's got high expectations of his people, but they all know what those expectations are. There's no variety; the standard for this waitress is the same as for that waitress. He doesn't play favorites, and he keeps it fair.

At the same time, Bob goes out of his way to take care of his crew. He asks a lot, but he gives a lot. The cooks in his IHOP are among the best paid in the community, and he tries very hard to ensure they get time off when they want it. He offers benefits, which is very rare in food service, and he invests a lot of time in his relationships with his customers and his employees. One employee even told me, "We couldn't possibly go anywhere else and be treated as well as we're treated here." That's the way to create happy, loyal employees, and happy, loyal employees create happy, loyal customers.

Communicating clear expectations and playing fair makes it easy to avoid one of the most common mistakes business owners make: having a favorite employee. Favorite employees are often friends or relatives of the owner. And I hate to say it, but they are usually very good-looking. If there's not a clear, evenly enforced set of standards that everyone is held to, that favorite employee can, and often does, get away with murder. This is a surefire way to create resentment among your employees. Even the sweetest, calmest, most wonderful people get ticked off when they see someone getting away with things that they'd never dare do. They may never say anything about how they feel, but you'd better believe they manifest their displeasure in other ways: slacking off, bad attitudes, petty theft—you'd be amazed what behaviors employees can justify when they feel they're being unfairly treated.

You need to walk the walk

You can't just tell your crew "We give great customer service" and then magically expect it to happen. As the owner, you've got to walk the walk, and let your employees see you giving great customer service. Your actions—whether it's helping a customer find the right product, spending hours researching the perfect investment advice for your clients, or carrying an order out to the parking lot—reinforce your words. If the owner's actions don't match the owner's words, then the employees know it's all a crock. They'll laugh, not where you can see them, of course, and figure you really didn't mean it when you talked about the importance of customer service.

Put your money where your mouth is. You can read a gazillion books on customer service, and I mean that literally; there are a gazillion books out there. (I counted. It took hours!) You could spend a fortune on training and having experts come in and tell your crew how to give great customer service. But I promise you, from the bottom of my heart, that there's not one single thing you can do to ensure great customer service in your store that's more effective than providing great customer service yourself. You do that, and your crew will follow your example.

Be trustworthy

We ask a lot of our employees, so we have to be willing to give as good as we get. If your employees don't trust you, you've got a problem. It's not a small problem, either. It's a huge problem that will destroy your store.

I think Kenny Abrams, the former president of Food Mart and one of my mentors, said it best: "If you want your employees to be honest, you've got to be honest." That means you can't steal from the cash register or pick a candy bar out of the display and eat it. You can't give your friends a "special deal" or take merchandise without paying for it. If extra merchandise arrives, unordered, in your latest shipment, you need to send it back or make arrangements to pay for it, and you need to let your crew know that that's the procedure for handling that situation. If you don't want your employees to do it, you can't do it yourself. And, on the other hand, if you want your crew to do something, you have to be willing to do it yourself.

There's a side note to this. There's no job in my stores that I won't do. I've cleaned toilets; I've picked up trash in the parking lot; I've dealt with the screaming, crying customers; I've straightened displays; and I've mopped floors. There's nothing I won't do in my stores, and I'd never ask my employees to do something I wasn't willing to do myself. You are not "above" your employees. There are no "little people" in your store. Each and every one of them is important, and each and every one of them deserves respect. Treating your employees with courtesy is an important part of making them trust you.

Be there for your people

Don't forget that if you want to have a relationship with the people who work in your stores, you actually have to be in your stores. This sounds like a no-brainer, but more often than not, we're in our offices, in meetings, or running off to trade shows. We're anywhere and everywhere but in our stores, where our people are.

Being in your store lets your employees get to know you. Let them see you in a good mood. Let them see you having fun. Too many times, our employees only see us when there's a problem. That can be intimidating. The boss can set the tone for the store; if you're cheery and upbeat, your employees will be, too.

In addition, the more you're in the store, the more you can be sure that what you see accurately represents what actually happens in the store. Any crew can put up a good front for ten or fifteen minutes, once a week, but if you're there on a regular basis, the real picture will come shining through.

Dave's Dozen

1. All the books in the world on customer service aren't as powerful as one real-life example.
2. Managing people is a skill everyone needs to learn.
3. Be fair and consistent and hold everyone to the same standard.
4. Don't play favorites!
5. Let your crew know what your expectations are.
6. You have to provide the same level of customer service that you want your crew to provide.
7. Be scrupulously honest and ethical; your crew sees everything.

8. The way you treat your employees is the single most important factor in employee retention: if you want to keep your crew around for a long time, you need to treat them right.

9. Be willing to do every job you ask your crew to do.

10. Treat your employees with courtesy and respect.

11. Be in the store to communicate with your crew.

12. Being in the store allows you to see more accurately what is happening in your stores.

13. The boss's mood is very powerful: try to be cheerful around your crew whenever it's possible and appropriate.

Chapter 11:

Know When to Let Go of an Employee

In an ideal world, I wouldn't have to write this section. Every employee would be fantastic and super-skilled, with a great attitude. Sadly, this isn't always the case. Sometimes we have to let an employee go.

When to fire someone

Part of being slow to hire, quick to fire, is actually firing someone. Every manager knows that the very worst part of the job is when you have to let someone go. When I have to fire someone, and I'd bet this is true for everyone reading this book, I can't sleep the night before. My stomach aches. It's just an awful, terrible spot to be in. I don't know of anyone who really enjoys it. (Well, maybe Donald Trump, but he's the exception to the rule.) Nonetheless, there are times when you clearly have to fire someone, such as:

> Someone is a thief, stealing from your store or your customers;

> Someone violates your sexual harassment policy;

> Someone violates your anti-discrimination policy;

> Someone fails to provide good customer service;

> Someone cannot perform his or her job duties to the standards you've set.

It's easy to get motivated to let someone go under some of these circumstances. No one's got a hard time getting rid of a thief or a jerk. It's the other situations, when someone's nice but inept, that are much more difficult. When someone just can't work up to your standards, no matter what you do to help them, you need to let them go.

If you don't, you're being unfair to your other employees. Think about it from the point of view of your other employees: why should they work so hard, putting all their energy and effort into doing a good job for you and your store, when others, who for whatever reason, choose not to do that, are equally rewarded? After a while, they'll decide there's no reason for them to work so hard, and your store will suffer as a result.

If that doesn't convince you, think about this. A store owner I know and respect was really struggling with his business. He had a dozen employees, all of whom he'd known a long time and really cared about. Two of them weren't pulling their weight: they weren't particularly competent, they weren't great at customer service, they weren't pleasant to be around—you get the picture. But the owner just could not bring himself to fire them. He worried about what was going to happen to these individuals when they lost their job. How would they pay their bills? How would they provide for their families?

I reminded him that he might want to reframe the question. Think beyond the two employees in question, focusing instead on the larger picture. The business was already struggling. If he kept those two employees on, and the business continued to fail, due in no small part to these two employees, then there would be twelve people who had paychecks in jeopardy, twelve families suddenly struggling to figure out how to pay the mortgage, cover the groceries, and fill the gas tank. (That's not even considering the owner's own financial situation.) Which was better? To cut loose the two damaging employees and save the entire business, or to let everyone suffer for the sake of the two? Phrased that way, it became pretty clear to the owner what he had to do.

You're in the same boat with employees who aren't happy working for you. They are never, ever going to be happy. They've got a negative outlook on life, and they couldn't crack a smile if you paid them fifty bucks for it. They're just not a whole lot of fun—not for you, not for their co-workers, and certainly not for your customers. You've got to get rid of these people. They're a cancer, and they'll destroy you.

How to fire someone

We're human beings, and we have compassion, so we feel bad when we fire someone. Luckily, there is a humane way to fire people. Here's what you need to do:

Do it in private

Bring the employee into your office. Never, ever, ever fire someone in front of their co-workers. It's dehumanizing and degrading. You wouldn't want someone to do that to you. Don't do it to someone else.

Of course, we live in a litigious age, and you don't want to leave yourself vulnerable. I recommend having another person in the office, preferably someone of the same gender as the person being fired, to witness the proceedings. A manager may be your best choice here.

Time it right

If you're letting someone go, do it early in the week. Firing someone on a Monday or Tuesday gives them an opportunity to start looking for another job right away. If you let someone go on a Friday, they won't be able to start looking for something else until the following week—that's two days just to sit and stew about the whole thing, which isn't good for anybody.

Document everything

People can and do sue over just about everything under the sun. You need to document everything that led to the firing: keep track of the behaviors, any steps you've taken to have the employee correct the behaviors, and any disciplinary actions. This is a good idea, even if your employment paperwork includes an employment-at-will clause. It is always better to be safe than sorry. Include all of this information in your employees' personnel folders, and retain it.

The aftermath

No matter how well you handle the discussion, you're acting as the bad guy when you fire someone. There's no way to come out of this smiling. Be prepared. No one's going to thank you for firing them.

On the other hand, you're likely to get some support from unexpected corners. Generally, after you let someone go, the remaining crew members will rally around you. Often, you'll hear: "What took you so long?" This is when all the horrible, negative information about the former employee will come out—often stuff that would have made your decision much easier, had you known it sooner.

Oh, and that stomachache you suffered while working up to firing the person? It'll go away soon enough, and you'll sleep like you haven't slept in days.

Dave's Dozen

1. Be slow to hire, quick to fire.
2. It's never pleasant to fire someone, but there are times it is necessary.
3. You have to fire someone who steals, violates key policies, fails to provide customer service, or simply cannot do the job.
4. A poor attitude is a perfectly good reason to fire someone; bad attitudes are contagious and can wreck your store!
5. Never keep employees on out of sympathy.
6. Keeping a poor employee on your staff is not fair to your other employees.

7. Always do the firing in the beginning of the week: this way they can start looking for another job right away.

8. Always do the firing in private: never in front of their colleagues and peers.

9. Protect yourself by having a manager in the room with you when you let the person go.

10. Document everything; you might need this information later.

11. Expect to be the bad guy; no one will ever thank you for firing them.

12. Don't be surprised when your crew rallies around you after the firing.

13. Remember: you will feel better when it is all over.

Ok, now I want you to do me a favor. Put down the book and get online. Visit me at

www.DaveRatner.com

I want to talk to you about the stuff you're reading about. And I promise, cross my heart, I'm not trying to sell you anything!

Part Three:

He Who Has the Funnest Store Wins

The sentiment is true: the retailer who has the most fun, exciting, enjoyable store wins. That's the store the customers will want to visit time and time again.

In this section, we're going to touch on what makes your store fun. Additionally, we're going to hit on all of those nuts and bolts factors that make one store more appealing than another.

Chapter 12:

Your Store

Location

I know, I know. You're shaking your heads. Great, Dave, location. Tell us something we haven't heard a million times before. But on this one, the conventional wisdom is absolutely, positively right. Location is the most important factor when it comes to making it easy for customers to do business with you.

Location plays a huge role in customer loyalty. If it's easy for your customers to get to you, if you're convenient to them, if they don't need to make a special trip to see you, you're going to get their business, and in a large part, that's by default. The retailer who has the best location wins. So if your customers have to travel more than seven miles to see you, move your store. That may sound really harsh, but research tells us that the lion's share of business comes from customers who travel seven miles or less to reach the store. So if customers have to travel more than seven miles to reach you, move your store.

There are exceptions to this, of course. If you're in a very rural location, where people are accustomed to driving miles and miles to get anywhere, seven miles is obviously not going to mean anything. But even in the countryside, there is still the issue of convenience to consider. If you're located near other destination locations, you're going to get more business than the retailer who's out in the middle of nowhere all by his lonesome.

It's one thing for customers to love you. It's another thing for them to actually come to your store. While we all want to do business with the local guy, if the CVS is convenient and the hometown pharmacy is not, we're going to go to CVS. We might be sad when the hometown pharmacy closes its doors, and we might lament the loss of small town, independent business, but the reality is that time is the most important thing to most of us. We make purchasing decisions based on what will save us the most time.

Some retailers have what are known as "destination stores"— stores that are powerful enough in and of themselves that location is only a secondary concern to them. Cabela's, Bass Pro Shops, and the Apple Stores, for example, all have this sort of magic draw that brings the customers flocking, no matter what. Some of these stores are so huge—three hundred thousand square feet or more, practically bigger than Rhode Island—that they obviously can't locate in traditional "prime" locations. Yet the owners of these stores still try to secure the best possible location, so there's a lesson there.

This is a lesson I kind of learned the hard way. For a while, Dave's Soda & Pet City was the only game in town. There were no other pet food stores in town. I was pretty much king of the castle, and let me tell you, they're right: it *is* good to be the king.

Then, in 1995, and before I could turn around twice, two PETCOs and two Pet Supplies Plus stores set up shop right in my backyard. I lost a lot of business. I mean a lot of business. Like a nitwit, I cut my prices. I thought if my prices were low enough, I'd be able to compete with these four new stores, and my customers would come back. It didn't work. Lowering my prices didn't bring the customers back. The customers who stayed enjoyed the lower prices, of course, but that wasn't really helping me.

It was time to figure out what was up. That's where the database turned out to be my friend once again. I had the computer generate a list of good customers who hadn't been in lately. Then I got up my nerve, sat down, called them, and asked what was up. This was definitely not the easiest thing I've ever done, but it was one of the most valuable. The customers were pretty forthcoming about why they weren't stopping in anymore: as much as they loved my store, the other stores were more convenient to them. They had better locations, so they got the business.

That meant I could drop prices all day long, and it wouldn't matter. On some level, there was absolutely nothing I could do to lure those customers back. Convenience was convenience, and I couldn't, with my store where it was, make myself more convenient. Location is always king.

It's not always about price. People, believe it or not, will knowingly pay higher prices in a convenient location than save a few dollars by going out of their way. Your customers have more money than time, and they value it accordingly.

Store layout

Independent retailers are in a unique position. We're not the same as grocery stores that have a gazillion and six categories, some of which are absolute daily essentials and others of which are specialty items that only get looked at once or twice a year. Most of us don't have the eighty-plus categories of a mass market retailer. We've got a handful of categories, or a couple dozen at most.

Yet we're all told to lay out our stores the same way, as if we're the grocers and the customer will feel compelled to wander through the aisles in order to get to the milk. There is no milk in our world. The sooner we accept that and abandon the "you've got to lay your store out this way" concept, the better off we'll be. I can't stress this enough. There's nothing, nothing, nothing in your store that the customer can't live without, get somewhere else, or order online. It doesn't matter what you sell. There is no milk. We can't afford to set up our stores as if there were.

Convenience is king for our customers. Set up the store to make life easy for the shopper. They want to be able to run in, grab what they need, and get out. Does that mean we put the best sellers within five feet of the front door? Not necessarily. You do want to draw the customer in. Your store should be engaging and inviting: if your customers have free time to spend, you want them to want to spend it in your store. However, things still have to be easy. Put your best sellers in a place where they're:

> easy to find
> near the cash wrap area
> strategically near related items you want to push

I'd like to take this moment to recommend Paco Underhill's book, *Why We Buy*, perhaps the world's best book on store layout. The concepts of laying out the store so customers can get in and out quickly, signing merchandise so it's clear how much it costs, and having quick, efficient checkout aisles all relate to the customer experience. The better you do in these areas, the more the customer's going to love you.

Be smart about signage

Signs are one of the most powerful and least understood tools any retailer has. I'd really encourage you to look into signage and what it can do for you; you'll be shocked! For example, merchandise that is signed outsells merchandise that isn't signed by up to 40 percent.

I don't know about you, but if I could increase my sales on any one given item by hanging a sign on it, I'll hang the sign!

The main thing I want to concentrate on here is how you can use signs to make your store easier to understand and more enjoyable for the customer. Here's the top three ways you can use signs:

1. Identify Sections
   Just because you know where all the merchandise is in your store doesn't mean the customer does. Highlight departments, and if you've got the room, break it down further from there.

2. Pinpoint Sale Merchandise
   A sign that reads "Sale!" or "New!" or "As Advertised!" will attract attention. For maximum benefit, point out what items are on sale and how much the customer is going to save.

3. Policy Signs
   Customers don't like to ask questions. Use signs to help them out by answering some questions long before they ask. Some examples are "Yes, you can return it!" or "If your dog doesn't like the food, Dave will eat it!" or "Of course we deliver!"

Have the merchandise your customers want to buy

It's okay to carry items that the mass merchants carry. There is a reason that large merchants carry those items: they sell. Customers want them. Can you imagine a grocery store without Coca-Cola? Of course not!

Remember, we are retailers. We are not the arbiters of style, and we are not our customers' parents. It is not our place to dictate what customers should want; our role is merely to provide them with the merchandise they want at a fair price.

Chapter 13:

Make Returns Easy

I keep coming back to the concept of returns throughout this book, and for good reason. Offering strong guarantees and making returns easy, even effortless, is one of the best things you can do to build your business.

You need a very liberal return policy. There will be those individuals who abuse it, but honestly, you're looking at a very small percentage of shoppers; most people don't knowingly try to put one over on you. Having a generous return policy makes it easy for customers to trust you. You're removing a large element of risk from the shopping process. They know that if they don't like what they bought, for whatever reason, they can always bring it back to you. With that comforting thought in mind, customers will buy more.

Make sure your crew totally understands the need to make returns seamless and easy for the customer. You don't want them to argue with the customer or give them a hard time. It's their attitude about the return that will influence your customer's entire image of your store. Make sure it's a positive image

Dave's Dozen

1. Location is the most important factor in making life easy for your customers.
2. Location is important even for destination stores!

3. If your customers have to travel more than seven miles to reach you, move your store.

4. Convenience is king: shoppers will go to the store that's easiest to reach.

5. Convenience is more important than price.

6. Have the merchandise your customers want to buy.

7. It's okay to carry the products bigger retailers carry.

8. You can carry products you don't like.

9. There is no milk: independent retailers need to lay out their stores with a focus on convenience.

10. Make sure your best sellers are easy to find.

11. Use signage to make it easy for customers to find their way around your store.

12. Have a liberal return policy!

13. Make sure your crew knows and understands the return policy.

Chapter 14:

Clear, Direct, and Effective Advertising

If you went down to your local Borders or favorite independent bookseller right now and bought every single book they have that discusses branding customer service, and then piled all of those books onto a scale, you'd have nearly a ton of pages in front of you. Branding is the hottest of hot topics.

Jeff Bezos, of Amazon.com, was one of the first guys I know of who really understands the whole idea of branding. He has a great definition, and I figure we'll start this chapter off with his words: "Your brand is what people say about your company when you're not around."

Advertising

This isn't a book about advertising; it's a book about creating customer loyalty. So why are we talking about ads? Don't most people hate advertising? Isn't this a surefire way to tick off your customers?

Well, yes and no. People hate advertising when it's bad. Bad advertising can ruin your business faster than anything. On the other hand, good advertising—smart, relevant advertising that makes your customer's life better—is the best thing you can do for your business. The right kind of advertising can, in fact, make your customers love you. The trick is knowing what the right kind of advertising is!

It's easy to pick out the wrong kind of advertising. One clue is the quantity: too much advertising, sent to everyone and anyone, whether or not they'd be the least bit interested in your products or services, is bad advertising. You're annoying the people who have no interest in your business, and overwhelming those who do.

Remember when we talked about the experience matching the expectation? How critical it is that every aspect of the time the customer spends with you matches or exceeds the experience they expect to have?

Guess what creates those expectations? Your advertising! The mental image customers have of your business, from the way the building looks to the way your crew conducts themselves to the way problems are resolved, is shaped, in no small part, by your advertising. That means you absolutely, positively cannot advertise an experience you can't deliver! The fastest way to ruin your brand is to promise something and have your customers discover that you can't back your promises up.

The power of targeted advertising

There are two schools of thought when it comes to advertising. There's what I call the shotgun mentality: plastering your ads all over the place, indiscriminately, the way a shotgun scatters shot. That's effective, but it's expensive. The other approach requires carefully targeting your advertising campaign. Identifying who your customers are, where they live, and what media they respond to allows the small retailer to advertise effectively.

Again, this brings us back to database marketing. You want to really work with the data you gather from your customers. Where do your customers live? Where do they work? When do they come see you? The answers to these questions help you make good advertising decisions. If the vast majority of your customers stop and see you on the way home from work, an ad on drive time radio could be a very good choice. On the other hand, there's no reason to advertise in newspapers that go to zip codes where few, if any, of your customers live.

That's the entry-level course in database marketing. What you want to do, if you want your customers to love you, is to ramp it up to the next level and really make your POS database system work for you.

Breaking customers down by zip code or prime shopping hours is a great start, but it's not nearly enough. By all means, if you're not doing that, start doing it now. In fact, start doing it yesterday. It's that important. But if that's all you're doing, you're selling yourselves, and more importantly, your customers, short.

Using your database to track customer purchases allows you to create categories. Using the Club Dave Card program, we've been able to identify customers who come to us for dog food, hamster treats, or aquariums. We know who sees us weekly, monthly, or once in a blue moon. We can pick out our good customers, our better customers, and our very best customers, and from there, we can extrapolate what marketing would be relevant and appropriate for them.

For example, as I'm writing these pages, we're putting together an e-mail campaign that will go out to our best customers. There's a coupon in the e-mail that's good for 10 percent off food, beverages, and fertilizer and one that's good for 20 percent off everything else in the store. Last year, we sent a similar coupon out to twelve thousand customers, and we got a 30 to 40 percent response rate. Customers want a deal, especially on the items they buy anyway.

Now, if you're a retailer reading this and saying to yourself, "I could never do that, it would kill my margins," let me explain that during the time the coupon's good, we take all of our specials off the floor. It doesn't hurt business a bit to do this; in fact, when we ran this campaign last March, the business absolutely exploded! (So I bet you can also understand why we're repeating the campaign!)

The key to this method is that everything you send to your customers must be relevant to them. They need to be interested in what you're sending. This isn't the place for promoting other items. Don't fall into the "suggestive selling" trap; while suggestive selling works great on the sales floor, it does not belong in your targeted advertising. I don't care what you have to do: tie a string around your finger, hang signs in your office, hire someone to hit you with a stick every time the thought crosses your mind, but don't send irrelevant information to your customers!

Relevant information, on the other hand, is great. Everyone loves a deal, and if you're telling someone that something they already buy is going to be on sale, you're not selling to them, you're providing a service. By the same token, if your industry faces a challenge similar to the pet food recall, use your database to communicate with your customers and let them know what the facts are. Letting my customers know that the pet food they were feeding their pets was safe was the best thing I ever used my database for.

Direct advertising

Direct advertising takes the concept of targeted advertising and brings it to the next level. Rather than aiming your advertising to a group of people likely to be interested in your business, you connect directly with individuals you know are interested in your products and services, with messages about the things they like to buy. I don't believe that there are any "magic bullets" in business—but direct advertising comes pretty close!

By mail

Direct mail can be tricky. You can spend a ton of money on direct mail and get very little response. Great direct mail marketers have told me about campaigns that get a 1 to 2 percent positive response rate, and they were happy about that. Let me tell you, if I ran a sale and only saw a 1 percent increase in customer traffic that day, I would not be a happy camper. For me, 1 to 2 percent is not enough to get excited about. If you're going to get excited about a 1 to 2 percent response rate, you're sending out such a huge mailing that numbers alone make the 1 to 2 percent response rate significant.

I don't have the budget to do that, and chances are, neither do you. Does that mean that direct mail's a non-starter? No way! I'm a great believer in direct mail. You've just got to be smart about it. The trick to direct mail is the same as it is with any other type of marketing effort: you've got to reach out to customers with offers that are of interest to them. Don't bother them with stuff that's not relevant. Only allow yourself to contact your customers when you know what you've got to say is a message they're going to want to hear.

Postcards are great for this. Let's say I've just gotten a great new wild bird food in the store. It's fabulous, it's fantastic, it's so great that flamingos are going to grab a cab and drive up from Florida to eat from your bird feeder. So what do I do? Do I send postcards to all of my customers, letting them know about the fabulous new wild bird food? Well, I could, but many of my customers could not care less about wild bird food. They don't feed the birds, they're not interested in the birds, and they aren't buying bird food period.

My wild bird customers, on the other hand, would be extremely interested. If I send a postcard just to these customers, highlighting the benefits of the new food, they're going to be beating down my doors. Throw in a coupon or price incentive, and the response rate goes up from there. On carefully targeted campaigns like this, I've seen a response rate of over 60 percent. That's the type of number I can get excited about. That's the type of traffic that makes the campaign more than pay for itself. That's direct mail working, and working well.

There are times you can use direct mail to reach out to all of your customers. We do a holiday postcard every year, and consistently get a 50 percent or higher response rate. However, the most effective use of direct mail is the carefully targeted campaign. The recent set of postcards we sent out for a free can of dog food garnered a 50 percent response rate among our customers who own dogs.

If you're worried about the logistics, there are about a gazillion companies out there who will do direct mailing for you. You'll want to shop around and find the companies who are willing to work with you at a price that doesn't make your eyes cross. Using a service makes this easy; you don't want to have your employees worrying with addressing postcards and making sure that there's only one mailing per household. Additionally, the service can do what's known as an NCOA for you. That's an annual survey, to ensure that the addresses you're sending stuff to are correct. You don't want to spend money and time advertising to people who aren't there!

By radio

I love radio. We advertise on the radio all the time. We advertise our store, we recruit employees, we announce events; if it can be done on radio, we do it. Why do I love radio so much? Radio's a great way to communicate your personality to the public. They hear your voice, your words, and your attitude coming out of the speakers. You can do more with a few words to let the customers know who you are than you can with pages of newspaper advertising. After hearing your voice and message enough, listeners start to feel like they know you. They begin to recognize your voice and mentally associate you with your business. If you've got a good radio voice, it's one of the best things you can do for your business.

Radio is very cost-effective for us, because we're in a relatively small market and we have four stores. If you're comparably situated, you'll want to check radio out. Smaller retailers trying to secure radio time in competitive, metropolitan markets might find the prices too high to be practical.

Radio advertising can also be targeted. A town may have only one newspaper, but it will usually have a bunch of radio stations that serve the same community. Each station has its own specific, niche demographic; by analyzing each station's demographics, you can pick the one that most closely matches your customer base. That's where you want to advertise.

By phone

Direct mail works, but there are other ways to reach out to your customers. Phone calls work, because they're unique. Almost nobody calls their customers. I do it, and it works really well for me. Here's how it works.

Let's say we're running a special on Dave's Cat Food. It's a great sale, sure to be of interest to my cat owners. I have someone in the office go to the database and pull up a list of phone numbers for my cat owners, specifically those who buy that brand of cat food. That list is going to be e-mailed to a voice and mobile marketing company called Smart Reply.

In the meantime, I record a message. It's me, talking to my cat lovers, telling them about the great deal we've got on Dave's Cat Food, when the sale starts, and how long the sale goes for. I send that message to Smart Reply. Smart Reply calls all of the numbers on that list, during the day, when most people are at work. My recorded message goes onto the answering machine, where it's heard by all of the cat owners, who now know to head to Dave's to pick up their supply of Dave's Cat Food.

This is probably my most powerful strategy, yet it's the one that most of you, right now, are shaking your heads about. "My customers won't like that," you're saying. Let me tell you what. My stores are set up in what may be the crunchiest, most granola-loving, socially-conscious, hippie-esque corner of Massachusetts. If anyone were going to complain about getting the phone calls, it would be my customers. These people are well-practiced in the art of complaining. Speaking their minds about things that make them unhappy is nothing new to these folks, okay? But while I'd estimate that we've called about a hundred thousand people over the years, no more than five have said anything negative about it.

How to make these phone calls work for you:

> Keep it personal and informal, like a message from a friend.
> Only call with relevant offers. We are very specific about who we call. Don't call your plus-sized customers when you're running a petites sale.
> Keep messages short and to the point. You only have twenty seconds.

> Don't do it too often. If you're running a "super special" every week, they're neither super nor special.

> If someone asks you not to call them, don't call them!

The nice thing about working with Smart Reply is that they take all the headaches out of the process. They have Best Practices reports you can reference, to make sure your messages are more effective. And more importantly, they won't let you inadvertently do anything illegal. Complying with the National Do Not Call Registry and other legal requirements is much easier with Smart Reply handling all the behind the scenes work.

By e-mail

We're constantly e-mailing people. E-mail is great: it costs so little to send, and more often than not, it's the best way to reach people. People check their e-mail constantly. They're online more than they're off. If you want to reach your customers, you need to go where they are.

E-mail communication is so cheap and effective that there's absolutely no reason not to do it. You need your customers' e-mail addresses; again, this is something you can capture with your POS system or by manually collecting them. If you manually collect them, have them all entered on a spreadsheet program; any community college should be able to steer you toward two or three students who can do the job for you. There's just no excuse not to have this information and keep it updated.

However, you've got to be smart about e-mailing your customers. Don't e-mail them every single day, and don't send them garbage. You don't want to be the Spam Master! The temptation is there to e-mail your customers each and every time you've got something they might like; keep yourself in check and only send e-mails when they're relevant.

E-mail marketing can also be used to direct people to your website. I've got to admit, we haven't perfected that yet. We're very good at generating e-mails that get people to come into the store. Getting them to shop online—well, not so much. However, that doesn't mean we won't figure it out eventually, and if a good chunk of your business is conducted online, you'll want to make that a priority.

What we have discovered is that e-mails get opened a lot more often if we include funny pet pictures. Everyone opens them because everyone likes to laugh. If you can make people laugh with your e-mail, they're going to forward it to their friends. Now they're marketing on your behalf!

If you've got it, flaunt it, part two

Earlier, we talked about what your store has that makes it stand out from all the other stores competing for the customer's time, attention, and dollars. This difference can be the cornerstone of your advertising efforts. This means if you're the only laundromat that offers garment repair, say that in your ads! If customers get free skate sharpening for life, go ahead and mention that in your radio advertising. Mention your distinct promise in all of your targeted advertising campaigns.

Constant contact

Right now, before you do anything else, I want you to put this book down, get on your computer, and go to www.constantcontact.com. If you're going to commit yourself to saying thank you to your customers, and plan to treat your best customers better, you need these guys.

Constant Contact manages your e-mail communications for you. They make it easy. You'll get a set of best practices, and they'll advise you on how to send the types of e-mails that your customers want to read. You don't want to be known as a spammer or the kind of clueless idiot who fills up your customers' inboxes with stuff they wouldn't in a million years want to read. Constant Contact can keep you from doing that. Go, sign up with them. They don't even pay me to say this— that's how good they are.

The other thing that's great about Constant Contact is they offer diagnostics on their service. You'll be able to tell how many people opened your e-mails, what links they clicked on, and what type of conversion rate—meaning customers actually buying something as a result of the e-mail—you're getting. They can make suggestions to help you create e-mails people are more likely to open and act on, which is really the whole point here.

In every single e-mail you send, you want to promise your customers that you'll never, ever give out their e-mail address. People don't want to be inundated with spam, and they know you're a potential source of it. You can't let your brand be used that way, and believe me, other companies are going to try to use you. I can't count the number of times suppliers and vendors have asked for my e-mail list, so they can send out messages "guaranteed" to be of interest to my customers. The most I've been willing to do is offer a compromise: they send me the message, and if it's really of interest to my customers, I'll forward it to them. So far, no one's taken me up on the offer. Big surprise!

Dave's Dozen

1. Every business needs to advertise: just make sure you can back up whatever you advertise.
2. Use your database to reach out to your very best customers.
3. Be smart about direct mail; focus on targeted campaigns.
4. Demonstrate respect for your customers by sending them appealing, relevant messages.
5. Keep your messages friendly, informal, informative, and short.
6. Use a service like Smart Reply to manage phone campaigns, learn about the best practices, and keep you in compliance with do not call registries.
7. E-mail communication is a great way to reach out to your customers.
8. Use a company like Constant Contact to make your life easy.

9. Make sure you're communicating those qualities that make your store unique!

10. Remember that funny e-mails get opened and forwarded.

11. Radio is a great way to get your personality out to the public.

12. Analyze a radio station's demographics to find the right station to advertise on.

13. Advertise all you want, but remember that your brand is the customer's in-store experience.

Chapter 15:

Don't Sell to Your Customers,
Give Them a Reason to Buy

To get people out of their houses, into their cars, across town, and into your business, you have to give them a reason to come. Some of this is marketing and promotion, some of it is the look and feel of your place, and a good chunk of the reason is emotional. Customers come because they like the way your crew treats them.

Selling is both an art and a science. Good salespeople are worth their weight in gold, because by listening to a customer and offering products that meet that customer's needs, with a highlight on benefits, they do more to reinforce your store's relationship with that customer than anything else in the world.

In this chapter, we're going to look at selling: what makes it work, and how to train your crew to do it well. We're also going to consider the role of community involvement in your relationship with customers. Sometimes, doing good is the best advertising you can do.

How to sell

I say that you can't teach customer service. People either get it or they don't, and there's no training you can do to fix that. The same is absolutely not true for selling. Effective selling is a skill, and you can teach people how to do it. The first and most important thing to understand about selling is that every single sale you make has to be a win/win proposition. It has to be good for your customer, and it needs to be good for you.

I learned this way back in 1979. This guy pulled into my parking lot, and you should have seen the get-up he was wearing. A hot pink sweater, bright lime green pants—this was an outfit that got attention. I mean, it was garish even by 1970s standards, and if you remember the seventies, you know that's saying something.

So he pulled into my parking lot, he got my attention, and he told me I had to listen to him talk about the new line of dog food he was selling. That man's name was Cliff Crosby, and he was selling Iams/Eukanuba. No matter what else happens in this world, I'm grateful to Cliff for one thing: he was the one who taught me how to sell. It's all about the benefits to the customer.

Benefits are what appeal to a customer. Benefits are what make a customer buy. Yet most salespeople are confused about the difference between features and benefits. With Iams dog food, the feature was the nutrition of the food. Iams, unlike most foods available at that time, was a meat-based food, featuring really high quality ingredients. They'd done lots of research before putting the food together to ensure that it had the optimum balance of fats and acids, vitamins and minerals for dogs. That was all good, but then Cliff raised the bar; he began explaining the benefits that were a direct result of all of Iams' features:

Dogs love meat, so they love meat-based food. They would eat Iams food with great enthusiasm. Nutritionally dense food means you feed your dog less, resulting in a lower cost-per-feeding than any other type of dog food. Dogs that ate Iams shed less. Dogs that ate Iams had brighter eyes. Dogs that ate Iams had more energy. Dogs that ate Iams were happier. And finally, dogs that ate Iams had fewer stools, which made for happier owners, who had less cleanup to do.

Bear in mind that Iams was a pioneering product. This was a much, much higher-priced dog food than customers were used to buying. Yet, because we could explain the benefits of this food, the customers bought Iams. We made way more money with Iams than we did with Purina.

For a while, it was a clear win/win situation. The customers—and their dogs—enjoyed all the benefits that came from using this nutritionally superior food. We enjoyed a higher profit margin with Iams than with any of our other products. There was supposed to be another win for the retailer, but we wound up losing, big time, largely because the Iams people lied right through their teeth. The original deal was that Iams would only be sold by pet professionals and veterinarians. Now, of course, you can buy Iams right next to any of the other dog foods at the local grocery store or the 7-Eleven. That promise of exclusivity fell by the wayside somewhere. It was nice while it lasted, but it sure didn't last long.

Anyway, there are some cool side effects to selling benefits. Selling benefits makes you the expert on the merchandise. At this point, I have a fair amount of expertise on pet food nutrition. That may not have been how I set out to live my life, but, hey, it worked. There's a clear spillover benefit here. Selling by focusing on the benefits means you learn an awful lot about your merchandise. At the end of the day, you probably know more about your products and services than almost everyone else in your area. You're the expert.

There are two benefits to becoming the expert. One is the impact it has on the sales floor. If I'm the expert on pet food nutrition, if you can trust what I've got to say about wet food and dry food and ingredient lists, there's a good chance I know what I'm talking about when it comes to dog shampoo and nail trimmers and training collars. It's easier for the customer to trust my recommendations, because I've established that I know what I'm talking about.

The second benefit has to do with your store brand. Becoming the expert means you become the go-to person for the media whenever there's a breaking story to do with your industry. When the pet food recall was big news, the local reporters were calling me for commentary. The same thing happened when Coke introduced New Coke: the phone rang off the hook. These media appearances build credibility with the public and help make them feel more confident about putting their trust in you.

It's okay if you don't make the sale this time

Are you ready for another story? You'll like this one; it illustrates a priceless lesson. If you come away with nothing else from this book, learn this lesson, and you'll be a happy retailer.

We sell a lot of fish at Dave's Soda and Pet City. Some of these fish wind up in aquariums, while others go into outdoor ponds. Increasingly, though, some people are setting up indoor fish ponds. It's a trendy choice, but people don't know a lot about them. How do they set up an indoor pond? What type of fish work best in this setting? What kind of pumps do they need? There are literally hundreds of questions you can ask about indoor fish ponds.

One customer wanted the answer to all of those hundreds of questions. He came in time and time again, asking Matt, one of our best sales associates, everything and anything about indoor fish ponds. He wanted to know about the liner. He wanted to know about the pump. He wanted to discuss, in detail, what types of fish would do best in that environment and why. Matt was there for him. He answered the questions, showed the guy examples of what he was talking about, and provided hours' and hours' worth of information. He had no idea if the guy was ever going to buy anything, and it really didn't look like he was going to, as the hours gave way to days, the days to weeks, and the weeks to months. This customer literally came into our store dozens of times without buying a single thing.

Matt didn't care. His purpose was to make the customer happy. The guy wanted information on indoor fish ponds, and Matt gave him that information. It made a real impression. When this customer was ready to buy, he bought from us, and he bought a lot. He spent a fortune on setting up an indoor pond, basing a lot of his purchases on Matt's recommendations.

That wasn't all. He was so thrilled with Matt, with the time, service, and information that Matt provided, that he wrote me a letter raving about his shopping experience and how wonderful Matt had made it for him. It turns out he was a businessman himself, and knew the value of a good employee—especially one who was willing to take all the time needed to make the customer happy!

Making the sale is not the most important thing. Making the customer happy is the most important thing. This can be difficult to remember, especially if you've got a customer like Matt's indoor pond guy, who takes up a lot of time and energy without immediately making a purchase. However, in the long run, you're way better off devoting the necessary time and energy into the relationship. The relationship is worth more to you in the long run than any one sale is going to be.

You see, this customer is the best type of customer to have. He's going to recommend our store to his friends. When people come over and admire his indoor pond, he'll gush about how Dave's helped him get it set up, and what an amazing experience he had. Building that relationship was the most critical thing Matt could have done, and he did a great job.

The same concept holds true in other fields. Let me tell you about my stockbroker, Mike Serafino. Now Mike will tell you he's not the world's greatest stockbroker. He's not Warren Buffet. If you want to move major shares on margin or trade esoteric options, he's not your guy. He'll tell you that, right up front. But what Mike does is get to know you better than anyone else. He spends the time, hours upon hours, really getting to know you, to understand your goals and your risk tolerance before making any recommendations at all. Making the sale is not what's important to Mike. Finding out enough about his customers to make the appropriate recommendations is.

In fact, if, during this research phase, Mike determines that he's not the right advisor for you, that his specialty doesn't meet your needs, he'll tell you. That kind of honesty attracts people, and is, in no small part, why Mike's so successful today. The point is, Mike spends all of this time learning about you first, without rushing to close the deal. Once he gets to know you, Mike will spend all kinds of time and energy researching financial options until he finds the absolutely perfect, totally individualized recommendations for you.

He concentrates on customer knowledge, rather than making the sale. That's why Mike Serafino transformed a small business into a thriving practice with an incredibly loyal customer base.

This concept doesn't just work on new customers, by the way. It's a critical aspect of your relationship with existing customers as well. Consider Fred Masters, from Master's Jewelers. When Ellen brought that watch in for repairs, he didn't try to sell her anything. He didn't show off new merchandise or bring out a pair of earrings he just knew she'd love. Instead, he focused on repairing the watch and reinforcing the customer relationship.

Community involvement

You can build a relationship inside of your business, but many of the most lucrative, profitable relationships any entrepreneur can have take place outside of the workplace. Getting out of your store and becoming involved with the community is the ultimate win/win proposition for independent retailers. The same is true for service professionals and just about every other type of business.

Become active in your local charitable groups: the Rotary, the Cancer Society, you name it. Seek out those groups that you believe in and that will help you promote your business. Anyone can be a butt-in-a-chair; you need to be more involved than that. Join boards, head committees, do some of the nuts-and-bolts work that keeps these groups going. This type of involvement is great for the community. It's also great for your business. Many salespeople build strong, profitable relationships by sitting on boards of committees and community organizations.

Say you're on the board of the local Cancer Society chapter. Every year, the Cancer Society does a fundraiser in which they sell daffodils. All of these daffodils need vases, ribbons, floral wrap, you name it. All that stuff has to come from somewhere. If you're in the floral supply business, and you're on the board of the Cancer Society, guess where that business goes? Even if you give the organization a break—which of course you would, being on the board and all—you're still going to realize some profit. At the same time, you get a big plus in the public's eyes for your community involvement. People like to do business with those retailers they see as being active and involved with the community. I think the best example I can give you of this concept is my friend Ted Hebert, of Teddy Bear Pools and Spas. Ted's got a great business, but that's not what sets Teddy Bear Pools and Spas apart.

Ted decided to market and brand his company solely through community involvement. He spends nothing on advertising—not a dime. He doesn't do TV, he doesn't do radio. What Ted does do is sports. Teddy Bear Pools and Spas has made a real commitment to community involvement, specifically through athletics. Teddy Bear Pools and Spas sponsors a gazillion teams. Cheerleading, hockey, softball, baseball, soccer—you name it, Ted's organization is involved in it somehow.

Little League is big in this part of Massachusetts, and I don't think there's a single league in the region that doesn't have a Teddy Bear Pools and Spas team in it. He sponsors the teams, provides the uniforms, puts up the pictures of the kids in his stores, the whole bit. This is great for the community, and it's also great business. What business is Ted in? Pools and spas. Who buys pools and spas? Families—specifically families with kids. At the point in their lives when most families are prepared to buy a pool, how old are their kids? Probably old enough to play Little League baseball.

Community involvement influences purchasing decisions. I'm not saying that the fact that Ted sponsors more baseball teams than you can shake a bat at is the only reason customers buy from him, but it's one of the reasons. When you've got a visible community presence and a reputation for doing good, the public notices.

That's why we do every home show in town, and attend every kids' fair. We want the public to see us out and involved in the community. You can even take this a step further by creating your own programs. Why not be the good guy? We do the Dave's Student of the Month program, with all of the schools in our region. Teachers can nominate a kid from their classes, and the child gets a certificate for a free beta fish and a bowl. We're rewarding the kids' efforts and reinforcing their value to their school and community, and we get rewarded when the whole family comes in to pick up the fish. The relationship we have with that family is established on a really positive note, or, if it's a family we already know, it's strengthened even further. During the summer, our local libraries have a summer Readathon, and you'd better believe we're there with two free goldfish for every single kid who reads the books! They've done their part, and we're going to do ours.

Consider what community organizations you can get involved with. For my store, organizations centering on pets and children were a natural fit. Schools and libraries can never have enough money, but there are literally thousands of other points on which retailers can tether themselves to the community. For example:

> A special occasion apparel retailer can donate gowns to military brides.
> A home improvement store can partner with Habitat for Humanity.
> A farm supply company can sponsor the FFA Fair.

Every business can benefit from community involvement. Talk with your best customers, and discover what they're passionate about. Most small business owners already have a pretty good clue about this, and if you don't, it won't take much to find out. Most people are pretty up-front about their passions.

Let's say a salesman comes to see me. Now, you take one step into my office, you're going to see about eight thousand pictures of my kids. Any space that's not taken up by photos of them is occupied by my collection of model classic cars. If you can't figure out something to talk to me about based on these clues, I can't help you. Use that type of clue—or simply ask your customer—to discover what causes are important to them. This is your opportunity to find a cause to support. When something resonates with you, when it strikes a chord you can't ignore, you'll know you've found it. From the smallest one-person outfit to the largest corporations, doing good is good business.

Dove's Campaign for Real Beauty is a brilliant example of this. By speaking to issues that are of real concern to lots of women, such as discomfort with prevailing standards of beauty, concerns about their daughters' self-image, and more, Dove found a place to connect with their target customer on a deep, emotional level. Dove's done groundbreaking work in promoting healthy body image in teenage girls, and at the same time driven their sales numbers through the roof.

That being said, you still have to provide a good shopping experience for your customers. It's not enough to sponsor the soccer league if your store is a dirty, inconvenient mess. Goodwill will only help you so much.

We can learn from each other

I make it a point to visit other stores to see how they are doing things. It amazes me how many business owners don't get out of their store. I'm not sure why this happens: it might be complacency or fear, but either way, it has to stop. You can't run your store living in a vacuum. You have to make a point of getting out of your store and into someone else's. Put your ego away for a while, and go discover what they're doing better.

You have to approach these visits with an open mind. Be a sponge: soak up what you're exposed to. Later, you can come back and think about what you've seen. Some of it may work for you, some of it may not, and other things might have to be tweaked a bit before you can make them your own.

Talk to your vendors

Vendors can be a great source of information. They're very forthcoming. It's in their best interest to help you: the more you sell overall, the more you're going to sell of their products, and the happier everyone is going to be. Ask them questions:

> ➤ What are other retailers doing to sell your products better?
> ➤ What do they do more effectively than I do?
> ➤ How can I improve?
> ➤ Where have you seen this?
> ➤ Who's the best sales team in your territory?

Be of value

The last, and simplest, reason a customer will buy is that we have something that is of value to them. Sometimes this is the merchandise—when you need a lawn mower, you're going to buy a lawn mower—but many times it's the relationship you have with the customer that's the real value.

Think back to Suzanne and her salesman. She's even said it: "It doesn't matter what he's selling!" The fact is that he has made himself of such value to her that she wants the relationship to continue. The same is true in any number of retail settings. Parents who come into Kiddlywinks find such value in Joy's understanding of them and their hopes and dreams for their children that they keep coming back. Our customers come back because we understand them and try to make them happy. That's the simplest way to be of value.

Dave's Dozen

1. While you can't teach customer service, you can teach people how to sell.
2. Every single sale has to be a win/win proposition: good for you, good for the customer.
3. Focus on benefits; features are nice, but only because they produce benefits. Benefits are what sell.
4. Focusing on benefits makes it easy for customers to perceive you as the expert.
5. It's okay if you don't make the sale this time.

6. Invest time in your customers; it will pay off big time.

7. Your purpose is to make the customer happy.

8. Community involvement helps you forge stronger relationships with your customers.

9. Become heavily involved with those organizations that are important to your customers. You might need to do a little research! Talk to your customers about it!

10. Research organizations before you decide to support them: you need to protect your brand.

11. Community involvement and sponsorship can support, and in some cases replace, your promotional efforts.

12. Always remember: your customer experience is your brand.

13. Get out of your store and visit other retailers. Ask your vendors what other stores do better: we can all learn from one another!

Closing Thoughts

Creating customer love: that's what we began this journey talking about, and now, at the end of the book, I think we've nailed down what it takes to make it happen in your store.

Unless You're The Cheapest Place on the Planet, You Need To Offer A Great Shopping Experience: this is quite a mouthful, but it's the essence of retailing today. The days in which we could compete on price are over. Today we've got to give customers a fantastic experience, so they keep coming back.

To do this, we need to *Hire Really Nice People Who Get It*. Nothing, and I mean nothing, you can do will influence the success of your store as much as hiring the right people and empowering them to do good work on your behalf.

Finally, remember that *He Who Has the Funnest Store Wins*. Every decision we make as retailers, from where to locate to how to answer the phones, helps create customer love. Paying attention to the nuts and bolts keeps the store moving smoothly. Don't ignore the details; they make the big picture possible!

Hey, we've done it! Here we are, at the end of the book. What a journey!

I have to tell you, when I started working on this book, it was a little overwhelming. I went to the bookstore and saw hundreds and hundreds of books for the small business owner. There's nothing in any of those books—and probably nothing in this one—that is revolutionary, earth-shaking news. All the basics you need to be successful have been out there for years. The problem is that given time, we forget. I hope this book has reminded you of some of those basics. We all need those little nudges along the way, to steer us back in the right direction and keep us moving forward. A little kick start, if you'd like, to get you excited about going to work again.

It's my sincere, heartfelt hope that you've found in this book some pointers that will stick with you, concepts you can use every day to improve your business. If they work for you, drop me a line at Dave@DaveRatner.com and let me know. (And if doesn't work, e-mail jimbob@hatmaill.com....)

Good luck!